# HOPE
## is the Struggle

## A Community in Action

Melissa Chamberlain

Elizabeth Garbish

Donna Leduc

Myrna Rose

Faye Wakeling

The Women's Collective of
St. Columba House

THE UNITED CHURCH PUBLISHING HOUSE

# HOPE is the Struggle
## A Community in Action



All biblical references are from *The Good News Bible: The Bible in Today's English Version,* Canadian Bible Society, Toronto, 1979.

---

**Canadian Cataloguing in Publication Data**

Main entry under title:

Hope is the struggle

Includes bibliographical references.
ISBN 1-55134-059-3

1. Point St. Charles (Montréal, Quebec). 2. Community development - Quebec (Province) - Montréal. 3. Community development - Religious aspects - Christianity.
4. Women in community development - Quebec (Province) - Montréal. I. Chamberlain, Melissa. II. St. Columba House. Women's Collective.

HN110.M6H6 1996      307.1'416'0971428      C96-931592-9

---

**The United Church Publishing House**
3250 Bloor St. West, 4th floor
Etobicoke, Ontario, Canada
M8X 2Y4
(416) 231-5931

Printed in Canada

# Contents

# Introduction

We are a group of five women who have worked collectively over the past two years to talk and to write about our years of struggle in our community. How we got involved and what keeps us going are the main threads running through our reflections.

Four of us are women who know (or have known) poverty first-hand. Myrna, Donna, Elizabeth and Melissa are long-time residents of Point St. Charles and have been involved in four different groups who are working for social change in our community. Faye has been involved in all of these groups in her work in the community over the past twelve years at St. Columba House, an outreach ministry of The United Church of Canada. She brought us together to discuss and write about our experiences.

The community of Point St. Charles is one of the most impoverished neighbourhoods in Montreal, with high unemployment, poor education, high numbers of single-parent families and enormous energy required for survival. There is a very strong community spirit in "the Point," as we all call it, and a long history of organizing together to combat the conditions of poverty that have always been here. People still look to the church for special family celebrations of baptism, first communion, confirmation, marriage and funerals but, as in the rest of Quebec, the church no longer plays a strong role in their daily lives. But there is a deep faith and commitment that lies just below the surface, and as women of different Christian denominations, we are trying to relate that faith to our day-to-day struggles. So we are looking for new language to speak about hope, our visions and our experience of how God is with our people.

In our discussions together we are trying to understand how change takes place, in ourselves personally and in our community. As poverty deepens and despair mounts, we are aware how important it is to analyse and confront the forces that work against us. Out of our experience in community organizations we have tried to understand and speak about the means by which change and empowerment happen. We have also looked at what we can learn from other people's writings and other communities involved in similar struggles.

We are all women in this writing collective for a number of reasons. First, in our community as in many others, it is primarily women who are involved in people's movements and organizations to work for social change. Women and children are the primary victims of poverty and we want to understand the significance of gender on socio-economic conditions. Out of our experience as women we are developing new ways of working together and writing this book is an important experience in itself.

So we bring our different gifts, knowledge and experience together, to speak of the "sources of hope" and the "work for social justice." We have recorded countless hours of discussions, have decided together what is important to put in our book and have reworked each section together. We have had sessions with people in the groups we work with and they have had input in the final write-up of work they are involved in. Our intent has been to produce something of value for ourselves and our community that expresses what has empowered us in our work, what obstacles have been overcome or remain, and the source of hope that keeps us going. We hope that our writing will be a way of sharing with other impoverished communities who are kindred spirits in the struggle. We also wish to communicate to those whose life experience has been very different, a sense of the strength, challenge and powerful spirit of a community that works together.

*Melissa Chamberlain*
*Elizabeth Garbish*
*Donna Leduc*
*Myrna Rose*
*Faye Wakeling*

*Point St. Charles, Montreal*
*September 1996*

# Acknowledgments

We wish to acknowledge the years of engagement of the people of Point St. Charles in their ongoing struggle for social rights and dignity.

We wish to acknowledge and express our thanks for the financial contributions from Urban Rural Mission of the World Council of Churches, St. Columba House, the Committee on Sexism of The United Church of Canada, and the United Theological College.

We are very grateful for the support, understanding and encouragement of Ruth Bradley-St-Cyr, the Managing Editor of The United Church Publishing House.

# The Women's Collective

*St. Columba House Women's Collective: Myrna, Melissa, Faye, Donna, Elizabeth (standing).*

**Melissa Chamberlain** is a vivacious mother of four young children whose experience of welfare and her life-long history in community work has given her a broad understanding of our community needs. She works in the "Point At Work" women's co-operative, is a member of the Women's Discussion Group, co-ordinator of the Women Against Contamination committee and has been a participant in the Worship Group. She is the daughter of another collective member, Myrna Rose. We can always count on her to tell it like it is.

**Elizabeth Garbish** is the backbone of the Point Adult Centre for Education. She also works as a Teacher's Aid, tutors in the After-School Program and participates in the Worship Group. She still finds priority time for her husband and four children, aged fourteen to twenty-two years, who live at home. The move from work as an office cleaner to community education has sent her life in new and exciting directions.

**Donna Leduc**'s wonderful, joyous laugh is known throughout the community. She is married, a mother of three children and grew up in Point St. Charles. She works in the "Point At Work" women's co-operative and tutors in the After-School Program. She somehow still finds time to volunteer as a committee member of the Point Adult Centre for Education and participates in the Women's Discussion Group and weekly worship at St. Columba House. Working in the co-operative has been an escape for her from the hard experience of being unemployed and on welfare.

**Myrna Rose** finds each day a challenge and a joy in her work as Coordinator of the "Hand in Hand" Program for adults with developmental disabilities. She is the mother of five grown children, including Melissa Chamberlain, and has known the humiliation of fifteen years as a single parent on welfare. Over the years she has found new strength through her involvement as co-animator of the Women's Discussion Group, participant in the Worship Group and a member of the Point Adult Centre for Education committee.

**Faye Wakeling**'s persistence and energy is what keeps us all going. She works directly with the Women's Discussion group, the women's upholstery co-operative, the Adult Education Centre, community coalitions and the weekly biblical reflections of the Worship Group and has been deeply affected by her involvement in the community. She is a United Church minister, Director of St. Columba House and is also engaged in solidarity work for socio-economic justice in the church at large and in society. She is a wife and mother of three grown children and two stepchildren.

# Glossary

**Action Watchdog** is a coalition of community groups in the Point whose mandate is to be engaged in the work of social transformation for a more just society through collective actions and education.

**After-School Program** provides homework help each day and a variety of activities such as arts and crafts, cooking, sports, drama, music and computer groups for elementary school children.

**Alternate School** is a bilingual head-start program for three and four year old children with parent participation and a focus on the total needs of the family.

**Day Camp** offers a month of fun and activities for 125 children as well as providing training and a first job to local young people as counsellors.

**Family Lunch Program** serves over 100 hot nutritious meals every weekday to parents with pre-school children. Each Tuesday, Community Lunch is open to all and includes discussion on current topics.

**Hand in Hand** is a daily program for intellectually challenged adults, training them to be more independent and using their capabilities to the fullest.

**Point Adult Centre for Education (PACE)** is the work of a local committee to provide popular education geared to community needs.

**Point at Work (PAW)** is a co-operative reupholstery project that offers a service to the community.

**Point in Print** is a printing training project that offers printing services and produces a monthly community journal.

**Teens Group** meets two nights a week with activities such as video production, drama, and rap sessions.

**Welfare Rights Committee** brings together welfare recipients for education, support, advocacy in the community and social activities.

**Women Against Contamination (WAC)** is a committee of the Women's Discussion Group that is engaged in research and testing for possible health effects on children from contaminatd soil in our community.

**Women's Discussion Group** meets weekly to talk, support one another, learn about social issues, and undertake to bring about changes in the community.

**Worship Group** meets weekly for an informal worship in which we discuss biblical texts in the light of our work and involvement in the Point.

# Guide to the St. Columba House Banner

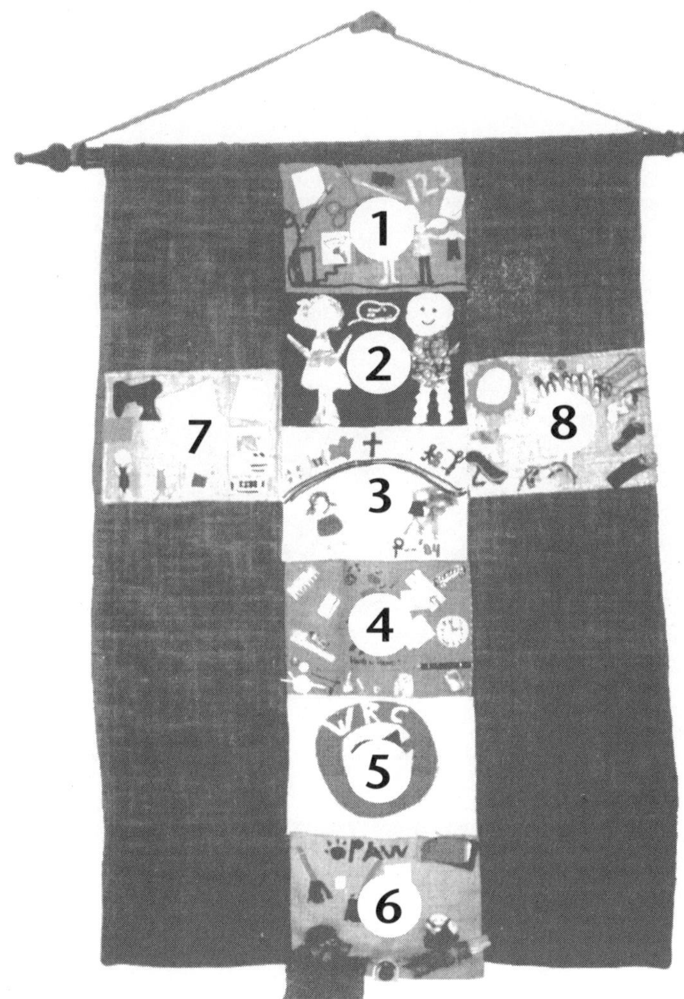

1. Alternate School
2. Family Lunch Program
3. Women's Discussion Group
4. Hand in Hand
5. Welfare Rights Committee
6. Point at Work (PAW)
7. Point Adult Centre for Education (PACE)
8. Summer Day Camp

# Map of Montreal and Point St. Charles

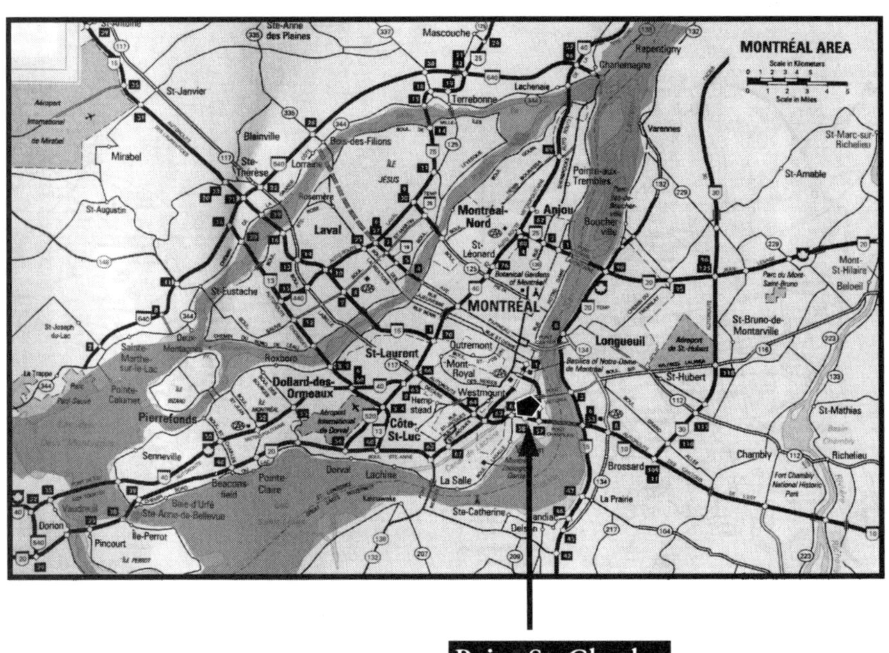

# HOPE – *What's in a word?*



***Out of the long, thoughtful silence, the response comes; "Hope is a big word."***

When we first discussed the possibility of writing a book together, Faye explained how important she felt our work was and that we had much to say about the problems that we faced and our hopes for the community. We had often remarked that we should jot down an important insight or write an article about the work we do, but writing a book had never occured to us. In our first working session together, we discussed what was important for us to write about as we look over the years of engagement and commitment. Faye suggested that for her, the question of hope, how people struggle, how they have hung in year after year, is really important to talk about and learn from, but that may not be what others felt.

Melissa's response was very powerful and profound. She said that no matter what the most important thing is for each one of us, "It is always hope that keeps you going. So hope is the good word." These words were not said lightly and the following discussion had a weight and significance that surprised us all.

Myrna said; "I think of hope as the support and strength we get from each other. I don't think that hope is just H-O-P-E, hope — a little word like that."

Then Melissa replied; "But you know it feels like it is right here, that you can touch it. But it's actually not. It is something very far away. But if it didn't feel so close, we wouldn't have it."

This became an important focus for us, in trying to describe or under-stand the contradictory nature of hope, as something that is so present and the very core of what keeps us going, while at the same time being "out there," elusive and beyond. As Elizabeth spoke of her understanding of hope in the context of her work with the Point Adult Centre for Education (PACE), she said; "Even when you get hope, it's like it's moving away! (this was met with a chorus of agreement) It's like PACE, for instance. We finally have the centre established and it's running quite smoothly, but I want more. I'm sure it could be better. It's hope, but it's also like you're hoping you can get a little more out of it and give more to the people. The needs are so great and you know you'll never fulfil all the needs. But its not greed, it's hope." Everyone is nodding in agreement and caught up in that sense of hope that pushes us on and does not allow us to be satisfied to stay where we are.

Myrna added; "You get really excited that you are going to reach this hope, whatever it is. You just go to grab it and, it is not that it jumps away, it is like it moves away just a little inch and you just can't get it!"

Melissa nodded in agreement and went on to say; "Let's say we accomplish something. But it is like Elizabeth said, you want more. So now it has gone a little bit further and you have to work that little bit harder now to reach it again. Or it's bigger — it is big. It's a big thing. It is not a little thing, hope."

There is a quietness that surrounds these last words, as everyone reflects on the enormity and importance of what we are discussing.

Faye says; "I am surprised the hope is 'out there,' because what I see you doing is so concrete, such as succeeding in organizing a new course for PACE, helping someone to make a breakthrough in learning, getting a good piece of furniture out that you are proud of...."

Myrna agrees but goes on to explain; "Let's say today I want to accomplish whatever and I do it. But it is never enough and the hope is still out there. I'm going to reach this goal, but all of a sudden I see a speck more that I could do, so the hope goes on. It feels like it is in me and then comes out, but never goes away."

At our next session, Myrna spoke of how significant our discussion had been for her in the intervening days as she continued to think through the implications for her and her work. Even though we had talked of hope many times over the years, particularly in the Worship Group, this discussion had a much greater impact. "For a small word, it sure means a lot. Hope is only four letters and look at the big meaning. As much as we talk about the hope and what it means for one another, it was reading over our own words in print that made it that much stronger."

It is as though hope is what calls people out, perhaps gives encouragement with the accomplishments along the way, but then opens up new horizons or challenges. Hope is *in* what you are doing, but beyond. We began to understand that it is not hope "out there" in the sense of being an abstract ideal, or something unattainable, but the tough nature of hope that is both in the struggle itself and the hard, ongoing work one is called to. Melissa expressed this in saying, "I find it is work. It's a struggle all the time. That is why I say it's out there. It's work, work, work."

Out of this sense of hope being the struggle itself came the question of how we identify or see this hope. Faye asked whether the sense of always searching to go further than we are, can mean that we don't always see the hope in what we are doing.

Donna stated that; "When you are inside, you don't see it. It is when you are outside the situation, looking in, that you can see something that gives you hope."

All of us had been together on a two-week education trip in Mexico last year (see Chapter 6) and had visited many community groups doing development work in very hard conditions. We discussed how we had returned with such a lift and an awareness of the hope that we saw in their struggle. But Melissa reminded us that some of the groups we met with had seen some of that hope in our work and that surprised us. "I could see it in their eyes that they were hoping they would get as strong as us. But they accomplished and did much more than we ever did as a group and I

*St. Columba House is more than a community building — it is building community!*

was embarrassed about that. They have struggled and struggled. If they set out to do something, they did it. Whereas sometimes in our Women's Group we just like to hear ourselves talk. This year we got a little bit better, but we've got a long way to go to get to their standards. Their life is a struggle for everything they do! But we didn't go to compare. We went to learn."

It is striking that in discussions of our work here we feel how heavy the work is and that it is a constant struggle. We found that the work of other groups engaged in struggle can be a source of hope.

We thought about how we had found hope in our lives and work, as we looked way back to those special times in our lives when someone or a group had helped us to see new possibilities. Our stories have the seeds of hope within them.

## Myrna's story

"We talk about a helping hand and I have often talked about the helping hand I have got over the years. But I never dreamed or thought of it as hope. But I think that lots of times, that is what it was when people encouraged me to do something. When someone tells you that you can do something then maybe you think that you should try it, for whatever reason. But at the time you don't sit down and think of it as hope.

"One of those times for me was encouraging me to work at St. Columba House. Kay Wallace was the Cook and she asked me to help out with the Lunch Program. I didn't think I had time and I had too many kids of my own to look after, but she really encouraged me. I was at St. Columba House because I had been bringing my son Randy to the Head Start program. You know, I never thought about it like that, but there was more to me than just coming with the kids to the school. She saw more in me than I knew I had myself.

"I always credit St. Columba House with the helping hand I got, but over the years there are some special people we have to thank along the way. I guess it goes back to the poem of the Footsteps in the Sand.[1] You know you can't do it by yourself. I *hoped* that I wouldn't always be in the rut that I was in and that I would have a better life. But I would never have done it by myself and I'm so thankful.

"I think that it was need that made me finally respond to the encouragement. When I say the need, I don't mean so much financial need, but the need to do something besides just being at home with children. It was another year before I was really on my own. Not having even enough to eat or to survive was a very hard situation at that time. It wasn't really a job at first. I just started to help around the kitchen at St. Columba, setting up the tables for the children to come in for lunch. l think it was the encouragement that Kay saw something in me I didn't see and that there should be more to my life. All I did before was take the children to school and then go back home. I didn't have friends, I didn't go to the grocery store, I didn't do anything.

"It was another five years before I got a job. I had been helping out in the kitchen and when one of the women workers left, I was offered her job. But it took a lot of encouragement and a lot of help from people to take it on. You know, you just didn't go in and do that. I never dreamed I could do it. I got married very young, at seventeen, so that I didn't have much time to do too much, not even to have friends. When you stay home for years, you really believe that you can't do anything else.

"As time went by I was given the job as Cook for the School Lunch program. I couldn't believe that I could be in charge of feeding about 150 children a day. You never know what you can do until you try. With help and encouragement and a lot of hard work, this job worked out very well.

"Then one day I was asked if I would like to start up a new program for adults with developmental disabilities in our community at St. Columba House. Again came the doubt — I can't do that! Now, looking back, I can't help thinking of Moses and so many others who felt they couldn't respond to something they were asked to do. But support came from others and because there was such a great need for that kind of program we found a way to start it. Now, fifteen years later, I often wonder how we ever did without it. The people who come to this program are so loving and giving. They have so much faith. It is a shared work of doing what God wants from each of us in love, faith and hope. Never a day goes by that I am not reminded of this great gift that has been given to me."

# Elizabeth's story

"You lose your identity when you stay home. I was eighteen when I got married. I was very young, too young and I think that if I had it to do over, I would have waited a few years if I knew what I know now. I was very quiet then and everyone else told me what I was going to do.

"I experienced a lot of what Myrna talked about as a child. I grew up in a divorced family and that happened when I was three. My Mom remarried, but it was to an alcoholic. So there was a lot of struggle for the kids as well as for my Mom. I hoped that I would never, ever get involved with someone who drank like that and mistreated us.

"I moved to the Point when Jason, my youngest, was three months old. I was quiet and I didn't know anyone either. I just took the kids to school, came home, fed them. I didn't have any friends. I was very quiet and shy, with no confidence in myself. Actually the first step was when I put Jason in the Alternate School at St. Columba House. You had to take your turn to be the parent in the classroom for one day a month with the teacher. I thought to myself, 'How am I ever going to do that? I won't even talk to the teacher. I'm too scared to be in the classroom.' I thought I didn't know how to handle children, even though I had my own and these were other people's children. I did go, but I was very shy and I did what I had to do.

"When Jason went on to Lorne School, there was only one day a year the parent had to be there in the classroom. I kind of enjoyed myself and I really liked that environment. The amazing thing is that the Kindergarten teacher said to me, 'You know, some day you are going to be a Teacher's Aid.' She said that to me way before I ever thought of it.

"I initially started to get involved through the Parent School Committee. I believe it was the Principal that asked me to be on the Parent's Committee. I said I had never done anything like that before and I didn't really think I should do it. I told him straight out that I couldn't talk in front of people. He said I just had to listen. That was where it first started, but I had been volunteering before that in the school. I think I just wanted to get out of the house.

"I got more involved in the Parent's Committee at Lorne School because I wanted the school to stay open. I lived just around the corner and I hated the thought of the kids going to school on a bus. That was the first thing that started me off.... It was practical reasons at first, but not afterwards. I still didn't have a lot of confidence in myself.

"When I think of how I got involved in PACE, I realize that it didn't happen all of a sudden. In the beginning a lot of us were involved, but that wasn't like me to take part. We had meetings at St. Columba House and divided into groups that worked on Alternative Education in Lorne School and Adult Education. I got involved in the Adult Education committee and we ended up going door-to-door in the Point to find out whether people were interested in adult education.

"Maybe it was just that I was always there at PACE. In the beginning, when we started the centre, I was a volunteer in the school a lot too. I was working at night at the same time. I just automatically went up and put the coffee on and got things set up. But that wasn't like me. So why did I do it?"

There are some similarities in Myrna's and Elizabeth's stories. They both needed to get out of the house and somebody else gave a push. Somebody else made the point of saying that they could do something. The people who recognized those special skills also went ahead and made sure that they told Myrna and Elizabeth about their potential. We realized how important it is for us to remember what an effect that can have. Often we need a real push from other people to get going.

Elizabeth recalled how much pushing she needed to stand up before the public meeting of the School Board to present the proposal for keeping the elementary school open and starting an Adult Education Centre. She reminded Faye of the first time she asked her to speak and she said, "I kept telling you I couldn't do it and I knew I couldn't. I was very nervous and you kept saying, 'Sure you can.' I remember those words — 'sure you can!' So that helped too, a lot. The first time I was so nervous I didn't even know what I said. I didn't feel I was that good, but everyone else kept saying I had done a good job."

Faye responded; "What was so strong about how you did it, was that it was clear that it wasn't easy for you. People could see how much it took for you to do it and how much it meant. It wasn't just somebody standing up and saying words that came easy or words that somebody else had prepared. That made such a difference."

She had done a wonderful job and had a very powerful impact. She brought hope to people who saw that they could fight together for the education they needed.

## Donna's story

"When my children were at the Alternate School I loved being involved. I always wanted to be a teacher. When the children started going to public school, then I got involved in the Women's Discussion Group. I was very quiet. I was terrified to do anything. You used to tell me — 'Make up your own mind, do what you want, make your own decisions.' I never decided anything without discussing it with my husband Fred. Then when I started going to the Women's Discussion Group, he would say — "*those women over there!*"

"I got involved with the School Committee the last year Lorne School was open. I came to one of the meetings partly out of curiosity and I saw that it was just women like me, concerned about their kids having a school. But for me it was a bit different, because I went to that school and now my kids were going there. That was my heritage. I didn't want to see my heritage go. To see it go really hurt and I think that's one of the reasons that kept me going.

"I had always hoped to be a teacher and I have very fond memories of my Grade 10 teacher. She was the one that said I could write. Although I have never pursued it, I do love to write. There was an incident that had a strong impact on me. The teacher had started up a library and someone broke into the library and vandalized the whole thing. She was so upset. She had really put her heart into it. I found her one day in the classroom bawling her eyes out and I was alone with her. I just rocked her and held her and hugged her until she felt a bit better. She wrote me a little note and I still have it to this day. She said that her bubble was burst and I gave her hope that day to carry on.

"I remember the first day I taught the sewing class at PACE. I was so scared I thought I was going to be sick. I thought, what am I doing? This is not me. But as I look back, I know that I had always hoped to be an elementary school teacher and I remember talking about that a number of times in the Women's Discussion Group. At first, I didn't think of the sewing class as being a teacher and that I was actually beginning to fulfil my ambition. I found that it gave me so much satisfaction that I was a part of what the students did. When we're talking about hope, I think of one student in the Sewing Class that couldn't sew at all and finally finished a whole suit. She was so happy!

"It is the same with the kids in the After-School program. One of the girls, Lisa, was having problems with math. I sat down and we went through it step by step. Finally at the end she caught on and she turned to me very excited, saying; 'I know how to do it now. Donna showed me.' Wow! I had a part in that."

## Melissa's story

"From a very young age, without even knowing it, I was involved in community work — starting at St. Columba House pre-school, to holding my first small, but hard-working job when I was eleven and twelve years old, washing dishes for the School Lunch program at St. Columba. I made the large sum of $2.50 a week and felt so proud of it. Without realizing it I was doing community work, talking about the lunch program to my friends and telling them they could eat there for just 25 cents for a whole meal. I remember singing grace and thanking the Lord for our meal. It is only as I grew older that I realized how important and special those years were to me and the hope it gave to the many families in our community."

Melissa had difficulty in school and shared how important it can be to have someone support or believe in you. She recalled; "I had a High School teacher that really used to make me feel good. A lot of the other teachers made me feel stupid in school, because I didn't read well. Mr. Anthony was a teacher from Trinidad and he always paid special attention to me. He was nice and no matter how bad I read — the words were always mixed up and I just didn't see them the way everybody else did — I was confident with him. He visited us at my mother's house and if I had trouble at the office he would come down with me to make sure they didn't get down on my back too hard. A lot of the frustration was because I was finding school so hard and he gave me a lot of support. It was difficult for me to keep up and I always got discouraged. He was always there for me. He said you're going to do well and you are going to be someone. He was the first one to give me encouragement.

"It is funny sometimes in community work how you always want to do more and it is never enough. We sometimes forget all the work and people we have helped and who have helped us along the way. I remember when I was a teenager volunteering as a coach for the Special Olympics for the intellectually challenged, the fullness I felt in my life when I was with them. These special people are so easily pleased and get so much pleasure from the smallest achievements. The smiles and love I always received left me feeling that I made a difference.

"As I grew older my work in the 'House' (St. Columba House) came to have a bigger impact on my life and how I would live it. Working as a Day Camp counsellor to working in the "Working Out" Job Search Project, gave me respect, confidence and maturity. The guidance from the staff and volunteers who were so dedicated to their work, showed me that the work was not only hard, but could be satisfying.

"When I was on my own with two very young children after a marriage that did not work out, I found myself on welfare and just another statistic in the government's eyes. I was not happy and found myself looking for employment. That is when hope re-entered my life. You guessed it! I was back at the 'House,' working in the *Point in Print* community journal project, helping to co-ordinate the Point At Work reupholstery co-operative and feeling an enormous amount of energy inside.

"My Mom (Myrna Rose), who is my mentor, gave me strength, love and a listening ear whenever it was needed. It is from her that I learned the importance of community work. Whether she knew it or not, it was her guidance, understanding and sensitivity in her work in the community that helped me know what I wanted to do with my life. She is a strong, hard-working woman who has left an enormous impact on everyone's lives she has touched."

## Faye's story

"I will start my story with my early connections to St. Columba House and the Point, because this community has really turned me around. I asked to do my field placement for my final year of ministry training at St. Columba House. I come from a working class background but had been lucky to have the chance to go on to University and then had moved into a very comfortable lifestyle. As I did my theological training I was increasingly disturbed by the growing disparities between rich and poor, both here in Canada and globally, and what I should be trying to do about it. So I came here to learn and ended up working with Myrna to start up the 'Hand in Hand' program for intellectually challenged adults.

"I was a real greenhorn, but working with Myrna, meeting with people here and being involved in community actions, began to open my eyes to both the injustice in our society and the strengths of the people in the

Point. I remember so clearly an incident that was a real turning point for me. We had developed a funding proposal to start up the 'Hand in Hand' program and were meeting with a woman from the Board of a major charitable organization (which will go nameless). I had seen first-hand the very special gifts Myrna and others in the community offered in helping people take charge of their lives, but this woman could only focus on formal educational credentials. Her comments were very critical and offensive to the people in the community and I could feel my anger mounting. She represented the judgemental opinions of so many out there and she wasn't even aware of what she was doing to the community people she was talking to. That day I saw so clearly what the stakes were and I stopped sitting on the fence.

"A few years later I was able to return as Director of St. Columba House and the learning really began. It has taken a long time as a 'non-Point person' to find my way, but this is really my community now. I found such strength and determination in the countless ways people struggle against unfair odds to make life liveable. But it was the women who struggled to keep Lorne School open and went on to develop the Point Adult Centre for Education that first showed me what hope was all about. We hit so many obstacles, but people never gave up. I have marvelled at the energy and commitment of women whose lives are already too heavy, to hang in. I have seen the power of community action and have been energized by it. People from the outside comment how hard it must be to deal with such tough situations all the time, but I know that it is here in this community that one finds the energy, the faith and a deeply rooted hope that changes everything. In writing this book together, we are trying to express what this really means."

We came back to the sense in which hope is so very present and tried to convey what this is. Myrna spoke of the discouragement we all face in confronting seemingly insurmountable problems. She also marvelled that we don't get more discouraged than we do. It is the "carrying on" that is the hope itself and the determination that there will continue to be hope. As Myrna said, "the struggle is the hope."

The question about what brings us hope continued to be so present in our discussions in the months that followed. Sometimes it seems like such hard work that it is difficult to see how this struggle can be called hope. We are saying that it is just hard work, but also saying that is hope — the hard work is also hope. The hope is right in the middle of such work as the struggle to keep PACE alive or the Upholstery Project going. That is the presence of God for us, the hope in the middle of the struggle.

But at the same time, hope is "out there," challenging us to do more and to hang in. It is this movement back and forth that makes it so strong. It is there, but it is not there. It is here, but it is "out there." It is the core of whatever you are doing and you have to grab that and shape it. As Melissa said, "It is the heart that keeps you going and the blood going and beating. It is right there and yet you are always struggling to *get* there."

# HOPE *is community* 2

*T*he Point is a poor community. There is no doubt about that. But there is a spirit and commitment here in this community that would be very hard to find anywhere else. People really chip in and help each other. When there is a fire, and there are many, people all help out by going around to community groups to find the help that is needed. There are so many people involved in the welfare of the community.

Generation after generation have lived in Point St. Charles. Most people have grandparents and great-grandparents that have lived here and those roots are very important. People came here from Ireland during the famine in the 1800's and from France, because this was an industrial area. Our ancestors built the bridges for Montreal, the Lachine Canal and the factories that encircle the community. There was lots of work! Much of the housing that is still here is factory housing built for the workers. People were working, but they were really exploited and there was lots of poverty from the beginning. The Black Rock that sits by the entrance to the Victoria Bridge was put there to remember the over 1000 people that died building that bridge and in the typhoid sheds along the canal. It was always a working class community, but now the majority of the people have no work.

So there is a lot of pride in both the history and the community spirit in the Point. It is one of the poorest areas of Montreal, but because of a long history of militancy and struggle it has survived with its own identity intact. However, it also has a reputation that is both positive and negative. We had many lively discussions about the blessings and hardships of being from "the Point."

## Pride in "the Point"

Melissa said; "When people ask me where I am from, I'll say the Point and sometimes people will say, 'Pointe Claire?' (an affluent West Island community). When I say, 'No, Point St. Charles,' they say 'Really?' (with great astonishment). So I answer, 'Yeah, that's where I'm from!' I'm actually proud to say that I'm from Point St. Charles. I think it is because of the reputation that it has and I used to feel like adding; 'Do you want to pick a fight?' (this was followed by gales of laughter from everyone). When we went to school, it was always — 'Don't pick on her. She's from the Point.' It was always like that."

Elizabeth added; "Even though our family has always worked, when people ask my son where he lives, he will say Montreal. He will never say anything about being from Point St. Charles. It is not that he is not proud to live here. He is just embarrassed to say the Point, because people have a misconception about what the Point is. They think there are gangs here and you can't walk safely. People from the outside who come to PACE are concerned whether it is safe to walk from the Metro."

There are no anglophone secondary schools in the community and so teens always have to go out of the community for High School. Even the Protestant elementary school has now been closed and those children are bussed to Westmount, the wealthiest community in Canada. These factors have made it necessary to find a way to cope with peer pressure in outside communities.

*The Point — A close-knit community where neighbours pull together.*

Melissa spoke about her experience as an adolescent and said; "People always knew, that if nothing else, the Point kids have that closeness. If there was trouble, it was true — all the kids from the Point stuck together, even if they had friends outside the Point."

Donna added; "When I went to High School, the only time I felt badly about coming from the Point was when there were problems with ethnic groups. There was a group of Blacks going up against the Point kids. That was the only time in my life I ever remember I was afraid to say I was from the Point. Besides that I could never understand why people thought that Point St. Charles was bad."

Faye asked; "Do you remember the women volunteers from the Reclaim program who were supposed to teach literacy at the Point Adult Centre for Education? They refused to come to the school because they thought our community was too dangerous, so they asked the students to come to their homes, outside the Point. Of course, no one went along with that and their teaching here was ended."

Donna recalled her experience in Sunday School at the Gospel Church on Ryde St. "One of the teachers, who lived outside the Point, told my mother when she came for lunch one day that they were worried about coming into the Point to teach Sunday School, because of gangs and violence. But they said that after becoming involved with the children, they went back and told the others that it was not what they had thought. There was nothing to be afraid of."

## Staying in school is hard

We discussed how hard it is for teens to keep up with others outside the community in schools and the tough memories some of us had ourselves. The drop-out rate is exceedingly high from the Point. Fifty percent of the population is functionally illiterate and the average level of education is Grade 9. There are so many factors that produce this problem and we are very concerned about understanding how we might turn this around.

We spoke of our concern that the kind of education that children receive in a community like ours is often second-rate. Many teachers feel that children are a write-off even at the elementary school level. The local school, before it was closed down, had been stripped of all the extra programs like special education classes and French immersion. So children were bussed out of the community for these programs instead of putting extra care and resources into an area that has so little.

Myrna said that she felt "Education is lower here and people have to work so hard to get what their kids need for school. It is not that the concern isn't there or that they don't try to educate their kids. Parents have worked very hard, especially over the last 20 years for their children's education and to keep our schools in the community. I think we get second-rate teachers. We have often been told that the children had to be put back when they got to James Lyng High School. The schools are putting the children down themselves."

Elizabeth spoke about her experience as a Teacher's Aid at Westmount Park School (the English Protestant school to which Point children are bussed) and said; "Many of the children don't have enough to eat. We are starting breakfast programs and lunch programs. A lot of the children come to school and haven't eaten. We see such a big difference now. Their whole attitude changes."

Many of us were very involved for years in the fight to keep the elementary school open in the Point. Our children had a daily hot lunch program at St. Columba House that would not be offered at the school to which  they are now bussed. So when the decision was made to close the school, we at least bargained to guarantee a lunch program for the children. However, institutions have short memories and the program was cut back this year.

With all the so-called concern in Quebec about school drop-outs, it is hard for us to understand how little will there is to tackle the fundamental problems created by conditions of poverty. High Schools do not seem to have dealt with food problems and there is a real stigma attached to kids who can't afford to buy their food in cafeterias.

Donna told us; "My daughter won't take a lunch to school with her. She leaves without breakfast and if she doesn't have money for lunch too, then she goes the whole day without eating. None of the kids take their lunch. So she doesn't want to be different."

Melissa spoke of a similar situation with her brother. "I found out that my young brother, Ivan, would go to school in the morning and then he would leave at lunch time. Or he would arrive just after lunch. Then I realized that it was because he didn't have money for lunch. The family just didn't have it. When I contacted the school, they told me that there were tickets at the school for those who needed them and that all he had to do was come to ask for them. I said that maybe he was embarrassed to come and that was why I was telling them about the problem.

"When I went to school, it was the jeans that were important — Sergio Valenti. I felt like a rag-picker. I feel like a rag-picker these years too, but in high school I especially didn't feel comfortable going to school. And I didn't understand how other people I knew who were poor could have leather jackets or Sergio Valenti jeans. I never understood that." It is one thing to feel that clothes are not important, but when you don't have the choice and are labelled by what you wear by others, it is very hard.

Elizabeth and Donna are tutors in the After-School program at St. Columba House. Many of the parents are not able to help their children with school work, no matter how much they would like to. Many families have so much pressure just surviving, that there isn't enough space or energy to give their children the academic support they need. The children who come to the program are really improving, but they need so much more. Many need to have one-on-one help and quieter places to work. When the children are bussed out of the area it is so hard for the parents to keep in touch with the school. There often isn't money to travel to the school and it is also very hard for many parents to feel at ease in schools outside of their community.

## Strong women

With all the pressures on families, it seems that it is usually the women who take on most of the responsibility. In our community 46 percent of the families are single parent families and the majority are headed by women. Women are more independent and stronger, out of necessity.

Melissa talked about the women on her street and said, "They're the survivors. You know, everything is left to them. Even if they are on fixed income, with their husbands or boyfriends at home, it is the women who are left to do everything. I see it daily now and it really makes me angry. It is terrible! The women have to be so strong and they have so much put on their shoulders. They have to be so independent instead of being able to share, even though there are two adults in the house.

"I don't know if it is like this in other communities, but I know that here in the Point it is the woman who has full control over the house. She has no choice but to be in control of the finances. She has to make sure there is money for food, have the bills paid, the kids dressed and the husband dressed. For families on fixed income, it is the woman who receives the cheque and that is how they survive. I find that the men just don't play a major role in the family because they don't know how to. So economically and support-wise the women are often on their own."

Most of the men really want to work and go out early in the morning to job banks, but cannot find stable work. They go to work placement offices like "Fairshare" and "Staff" at 5:30 in the morning hoping to get a job for the day, at minimum wage. We recalled how this was just like the passage in the Bible about the workers waiting in the marketplace all day to be hired.[2] Work has always been the man's contribution to the family and without it, most of them have been unable to shift to new ways to relate within the family.

The lack of food is such a serious problem for so many people in the community. Like other cities across the country, Food Banks have sprung up to try to meet the desperate need for food and, even though we all see this as band-aid activity, it is a necessity. We are shocked by the increasing numbers of people who need food and very concerned that each week we see people lining up who have never had to ask for help before. We felt that no matter how sensitive one tries to be, there is no way to give out food that is not degrading to those who receive it.

Donna remarked that, "Now it seems that there are line-ups everywhere at all times of the month. It used to be just towards the end of the month." Even at the first of the month when people get their welfare cheque, after they have paid their rent, hydro, heat, telephone, there is nothing left for food. There used to be a lot more food programs for children in schools than there are now. The milk program at school and the hot lunches provided in areas of poverty are being cut back. The children from the Point are bussed to Westmount and, even though the majority of the children in the school qualify for a subsidized lunch program, it has been discontinued because the family income statistics include the wealthy minority in that school.

Myrna has been involved in helping with a Collective Kitchen, which has been an innovative way to face the food problem. She is impressed with the results she has seen and exclaimed very enthusiastically; "Collective Kitchens are great! They help people pool their money together, make meals, learn new ideas and find nutritious ways to feed their families. Plus it is also people getting together talking about issues that are important. As people talk about their situation and the system they are trying to survive in, they find that they are not the only ones in that situation. It can be very degrading if you think that you are just not managing your money right." In addition to providing inexpensive, nutritious meals for their families, the women find that they are not alone.

Another real challenge in our community is the relationship between the English and the French. In Point St. Charles, 60 percent of the residents are francophones and 35 percent anglophones (30 years ago these numbers were reversed). We talked about how historically the railway tracks always separated the French from the English, but that has really changed recently. In spite of differences and some tension, we all come together for actions or community causes. Elizabeth recalled that "there used to be more fighting between the French and English children, but there doesn't seem to be much of a problem now. There is French and English in all the schools now and that makes a difference."

However, there are a lot of francophones that don't speak English and anglophones that don't speak French. It is hard to function together on committees because you might understand the other language, but not enough to express yourself and really participate. Myrna remarked; "But I am very comfortable here. I will speak French when I can, but even if we don't always understand every word, we find a way to communicate." We are trying to find new ways to meet and work together.

## God is *in* the struggle

There are many churches in the Point, but for the majority of residents, organized religion doesn't have a very profound effect on their lives now. The churches are important to the older generation, but others do not find they are getting out of it what they want.

Melissa attends church irregularly and explained; "I know myself, being a younger mother, I do not go to church for the social aspects. I go for the religious aspects and there are no social events whatever. I just go to feel good and I always feel good when I leave church. I like my church in that sense, but the sermons are very boring and they're the same. But I've always said that when the church starts changing, the people will start going. They're in their old ways and I don't see them changing in the near future."

We all agreed that for traditional reasons the church is important for weddings, baptisms and funerals. Many in the community are Catholic and since the Catholic Church does not recognize civil marriages, people are married in the church. In Quebec, births were officially registered through baptism, but that has recently changed and you have to register the baby yourself at City Hall. We wondered if that would produce changes for young families in the future.

Myrna spoke very emphatically saying; "I think church is very important. I just don't find the church gives me what I need. I go there and listen to the sermon, but I want more than that. Maybe if people participated in the service it would help. I don't want them preaching to me, but I want them to help me understand what they mean by what they are reading. We do it different when we have our worship services at St. Columba House. I am not blaming it on that, but I have a whole different outlook now on what I want. When I come home from church, I'm flustered. Really, it comes on like *'you have to do this! This is what was stated! God wants you to do that, that way!'*" she says, hitting the table as she speaks.

Melissa disagreed; "I don't find St. Gabe's (St. Gabriel Roman Catholic Church) that way. I find it very mellow. If you really listen now, they even talk about the times getting harder and that things have to change. But I find that the church itself hasn't changed and the church is not very helpful in the community. They give food and furniture if needed, but only to people who belong to the parish — not just a person who has needs. I still look up to my priest and if I needed something, he would be there to help me. But I don't feel that the church is there for us in our struggles."

Myrna went on to say; "I think that a Christian community, or a church in a community is very important. They have the power to do so much. People are willing with open arms to do things that the church wants. They have to do constructive things within the church for the people to go, that are interesting for the people and makes them feel more involved. Not fund-raisers to have a new paint job, or cushions or satin altars or stuff to buy for the church — but something that is going to help the community and help the church too. It is a two-way street. If you get involved in the community to do a special project that the community wants, they profit by doing a good deed and people will see that they are supportive of the community. It works both ways." At this point Myrna was becoming completely exasperated and finally ended by saying, "I am getting flustered! I don't want to talk about this any more!"

We had all expressed great disappointment and frustration that the local churches are not the place where we find support and encouragement for all the work we have been involved in to change the hard conditions that face people. This does not mean that we do not have faith. Our faith is at the core of our community involvement. As Myrna explained; "You can't separate it. The work is the life and the life is the work. This is church for us!"

We see St. Columba House as a church in action. For us, and many in the community, this is a place where we feel God's presence, where all people are welcome and where they gather to celebrate, to eat, to worship and support each other. Melissa added; "This is where God touches every one of us. I think God just means everything to everybody. I don't know anybody — Catholic, Protestant, whatever — that doesn't have faith. They *really, really* want so much. God is still giving them hope, faith, and that little extra to carry on. But people are not finding ways to express it. They are keeping it in themselves, in their families."

Myrna agreed; "They have faith. The majority of people have faith — in survival, in life, in their children."

This was a very heavy discussion and after a long period of quiet Donna said; "It just kind of hit me. The church preaches a heavenly God, when what we need, and I think people are looking for, is an earthly God. I think that for me, that is what I found in the Worship Group. I found a God that is not "up there" looking down, scratching his or her head. God is not looking down at this mess but God is in the struggle and God is trying to give some kind of support."

After looking at what our community is like, with all its strengths and weaknesses, we asked ourselves what makes it a good place for us to live. For all of us, it is the support that is here and how easy it is to know people. In thinking about the strengths of the community, Melissa began to talk about some people who have made such a difference here. "Rolly is very proud of the Point and the community. He puts great pride into his work. All these years he has put into the work here at St. Columba House in the Welfare Rights Committee! He is very proud of who he is and he doesn't look down on himself as a welfare recipient. He is a people person and he really helps people. He speaks of his friends and his family who grew up here and he is very proud."

A few months after this discussion, Rolly died suddenly of a heart attack at age 45. People from the whole community came together for his funeral at St. Columba House — Protestants, Catholics, non-believers and other faiths. Rolly had no immediate family and it was so striking to us all that we, St. Columba House and the organizations he worked with, were truly family. It was one of those special times, when in the midst of grief, you see more clearly, the meaning of "Amazing Grace," that presence of God in our midst in the fight against injustice. We spoke of the hope that he brought to so many people through his work against the dehumanising welfare system and how bound together we are as a community of God's people in this work for social change. As we joined hands to sing "We Shall Overcome" at the close of the service, it was like a deep understanding of the hope that undergirds us and a commitment to carry forth this work.

The welfare system is a trap that neither encourages or allows people to find ways to make it on their own. There are families that have been on welfare for generations and it is hard to know how that cycle will be broken.

Donna shared her concern that "the kids aren't given the tools to do something better or the parents aren't. They don't have any resources they can go to and try to better themselves. I know that as parents, we always want better for our children. But if you are on welfare, how can you give your child a half decent education? I have Jessica in school and she will go to college next year. I'll have to buy her books and everything and I'm already worried about it. College isn't supposed to be expensive compared to university, but if you have a family that is on welfare or on low income it is very hard, unless your child can work and supplement it by saving money."

Elizabeth replied; "Some people don't seem to have that energy or drive or something to show their children a different way. Money has a lot to do with it. It is the same with a family on low income. We all want better for our children, but if we don't show them how to get it, where are they going to learn? I would have gone further along. I stopped at high school because there was no money at all to go on. I would have loved to go on at that point, but there was no way. I got married instead. But I was one of the lucky ones who got married to somebody who helped me along too. I mean, not totally in the beginning, when he felt my place was in the home too, like his mother. It does pass down. I don't know, but there must have been something in me. I have an extraordinary mother who pushed and let us know that we could do whatever we wanted. However the money wasn't there and you couldn't do *any* thing that you wanted."

Faye expressed her concern about the limitations people face and that "sometimes the vision of what we could do isn't very far beyond what we have seen in our families. We have seen this in the Women's Discussion group. The dreaming stops pretty close to home. It's tough, because it is not just the money, but whether we can imagine we could do it differently."

Myrna replied; "I got the feeling from some of our discussions lately, that people are just giving up. People have given up even trying to get jobs. I think that is what has made me feel so bad the last couple of meetings. You look around the table at the Women's Group and if you ask whether anything good has happened in the past week, there is so little."

## Poor, living in poverty, low income or impoverished?

Although we began talking about our community as a "poor" community, we are not satisfied with what this word says or means to others. It feels like such a put-down to call people poor and yet it is so important to deal directly with what poverty is and does. Some of us feel that using the words "people who live in poverty" is not as bad as "poor," but we still don't really like it.

Melissa doesn't see a problem with using the word poor and she explained; "Poor to me doesn't mean that I am unclean. I mean to me personally. That is why I use poor. Poor to me is somebody who struggles, who does without, who just cannot make it in this world, in this society."

"I often use 'low-income,'" Faye said, "but I know it doesn't say the same thing. People on low-income have a tough time to make it. They have to watch every penny, but there is a sense that they have an income. People don't even consider welfare an income. They don't call it an income, even though it is. I use 'low-income' because other words can be insulting, but it doesn't really name poverty."

Myrna agreed; "It is not powerful enough either. But when I was away one time at a conference, the word poor was used and it really offended people."

We tried to find a way to express what must be said without offending people. Faye suggested that "when we use poverty it doesn't sound as though you are defining somebody by it but that it is a condition that you are forced to live in. People who live in poverty are not necessarily defined as 'the poor.' However, there are poor people throughout the world and we want to make connections with them — strong and political connections with the poor.

"When I met with the Mayan church people in Guatemala recently, they had a whole day of reflection on their work and what they are doing. The animator at one point used the Spanish word that means 'impoverished.' He said that he used it because *'im-poverished'* means that somebody else has done it to you. He sees it as a political way to deal with poverty. Impoverished is an active word. It is not a condition, but it is something imposed on you. It is like somebody has been cheated and been impoverished. I thought it was very helpful."

Myrna replied; "It doesn't sound overwhelming. It doesn't sound like a nice way to say it, but it doesn't sound dirty. I guess that is what bothers me about 'poor.' When we say it, it sounds dirty."

"As soon as you said the word impoverished," Donna said, "I thought, here is another ucky word. That was my first thought. But when you started to explain it, I loved the definition. I would have a much easier time with impoverished than to say that I am poor. I am thinking that poor does not give that person dignity. If anything, it strips it away. I am thinking that in that situation someone could say with at least some dignity, 'I am impoverished,' because it is a situation that is inflicted on them. They didn't ask to be put there."

Then Myrna said very forcefully; "Well, I am going to say it — what I really think! I don't mind using impoverished because now that we talked about it, we know what it is. But what about other women? They won't know what it means. How are they going to feel? We want to make sure we use language people understand."

We realize that this is a very difficult discussion that we will have to continue to work on. We don't like to use "people who live in poverty" and we don't like "the poor." "The poor" used to be used as a kind of rallying word to identify people who have been exploited and people who have rights that are not respected. Because of other people's opinions that to be poor is something dirty, it is not possible to use the word without it feeling judgemental. To a lot of people, if you are poor you are dirt, the scum of the earth. We know that it serves a lot of people's purposes to support that idea and to imply that people who are "impoverished" are of less value. There are too many bad memories of this kind of judgement!

Myrna thought back to her own hard experience of raising five children as a single parent on welfare and said; "I think it stayed with me. I'll never forget when someone brought me a food basket and said, 'Oh look at those kids, how clean they are!' What did they think they were going to see?"

Whatever word or words we choose to use, poverty is the major problem in our community. Fifty-five percent of the community is jobless and since Montreal is the city with the highest unemployment in the country, there is no promise of change in the near future. Welfare income in Québec is less than 50 percent of the poverty line and each month there are further cut-backs or punitive conditions. So how do people survive? What happens to a community that is pushed deeper and deeper into poverty? What resources do we have to fight back or to find other solutions that will offer hope and dignity? The various ways we are engaged in this long-term work and the sources of hope for our community are the subject of this collective writing.

## Fighting to survive

We have many strong community organizations that continue to work and fight for economic development, the rights of welfare recipients, affordable decent housing, accessible education, legal rights, ecological concerns, youth programs and centres and resources for women.

However, in the meantime, we are confronted with the problems and changing values in a community where people are fighting to survive. This means that people are forced to use the system in any way they can to put food on the table. It is not considered dishonest not to declare babysitting money or the income from occasional labour jobs, when after a very low minimum, the earnings will be deducted dollar for dollar off the welfare cheque. People work on the side because they have to make extra money to survive. Many families pay two-thirds of their income on rent and heat, leaving almost nothing for other basic essentials. Line-ups at food banks continue to increase and what was once considered a basic necessity in our society — a telephone — has become too expensive for many families.

Into this monthly struggle to make it, there are always the unexpected crises and needs. For example, if your washing machine breaks down, there is no laundromat nearby and you have no car to take your children's laundry, what are the options?

If you are on welfare you cannot get a loan from a bank or credit company and you cannot get a credit or lay-away at any regular department store. The majority of people in our community get in touch with a "Home Merchant" or a "Sales Merchant" (called a variety of other names we have decided not to print) to get them through the crises. He will either pick you up and take you to a store to purchase what you need or he will phone ahead and tell the store that he is covering a line of credit of a certain amount. You pay about 40 percent interest and the stores you have to shop in are often very expensive. You can't shop around for a sale somewhere, but have to go where you are sent. So the whole system is very expensive and the longer you take to pay, the higher it costs because of interest. If you are on welfare, you may only have to pay $25 a month, but it never gets paid off.

We estimate that about 80 percent of the people in the community have used Home Merchants because they have no other choice. It means that when you are broke you can go shopping for what you need — a fridge, a stove, beds for the kids, clothing, whatever. There is no way you could ever save up for these when your income is 50 percent of the poverty line. But it also becomes an accepted way to manage in the community and there doesn't seem to be any solution to mounting debts. This is a real concern for us with our children as they grow up. We try to discourage them from falling into the same traps, but they will probably have to learn on their own.

Myrna recalled; "When we were younger, we never had the things that other children got. It didn't have to be a lot. I just wanted something like the other children got. I think it goes with me never thinking I am going to have enough food. I always feel guilty at Christmas too that I couldn't get things for my children when they were younger and so I buy much more than I should. Not having enough for a long time does that to you and you just can't erase it."

Donna talked about how it was in her family and said; "We went to a merchant once. He was very nice, but that was the last time. We are never going to get in debt again. I grew up with the principle that you save your money and if you don't have it, you do without. I have brought the kids up that way too. If you don't have, you do without."

We began to talk about the availability of "hot stuff" (stolen goods) in the community and this has been a very difficult subject for us to deal with. It is having an effect on the community and is a real problem for all of us as we consider the effects on our children.

Melissa explained; "I think that the people on my street look at it more with a sense of relief that they can get something that they need at a cheaper price and then they have more money for something else. As things get worse, it is going to get worse. I see people getting poorer. More and more people are buying hot stuff now. Most of the people who go around selling are not teenage kids. They are adults with families who are doing it to provide for their families."

We had great difficulty deciding how much of our discussion we were willing to share. But we felt that it is a part of our reality and so we should try to deal with it together. We have disagreements among us, but see it as a very important issue. How are we going to deal with it in our families? What does it mean when a whole community tolerates it? These are some of our comments:

"None of us want our children to be buying hot stuff or know about it. So if it gets more and more out there and our children know about it, then in the long term what is going to happen?"

"In our community there are no jobs and no money. Then people get into a situation where they feel they don't have a choice and so this is how they manage."

"If I buy something hot, I have to live with that. I have to settle my own conscience, whatever way I do that."

"I would never have one hesitation about someone whose kids were starving, going and stealing. But the situation of many people buying hot stuff is not necessarily that. It is also tied to the problems of us needing more and more, like the kids with the right kind of running shoes. But when a family makes the choice that your kids will learn to do without, it is very tough on them at school when they don't have what the others have."

"It is a hard decision. My kids did without so many things."

"Who am I now to sit here and think what is right or wrong? Not that I didn't feel bad when I did it, when I bought something that was hot before. I always felt guilty. But all of a sudden it seems that we are talking about what other people do and why they do it. But who am I to sit here and say what people should do who are really stuck? I don't want to come across as judgemental, but on the other hand, I don't want to lose the importance of what we are talking about."

"I don't blame them, I blame the situation that they are in. That is what I blame."

"In a context where you can't make it, what is right or wrong is very different, but it is a slippery slope that gets you into all kinds of other trouble."

This has been a very tough discussion for us and we decided to read from a book that Faye thought might give us some ideas to bounce off. We read Chapter 5, "Beating the System" and Chapter 10, "The Bottom Line" from a book called *Monday Morality: Right and Wrong in Daily Life.*[3] It didn't seem to resolve anything, but it certainly provoked quite a reaction!

We felt that the book had not dealt with the situation of people in dire need and that the emphasis seemed to be on individual morality. It didn't seem fair if each individual person had to deal with this just as their own personal problem. We never treat anything else in the community as just our own personal problem. We always look at how taxation, the welfare system and the lack of jobs affects us all. We look at the effects of increasing poverty on health, the ability to learn, the lack of dignity and the exhaustion of the struggle to survive. But whether people buy hot stuff to survive is never brought up in the community as an issue. There just seems to be no way to handle it — yet.

We are left with many questions concerning conflicting values. What are real needs? Are these things necessary to the point that I will be ready to risk the beliefs that I live by? We agreed that there is a serious danger if a practise becomes so accepted, that we stop asking these questions. Through our discussions together we have looked at the possible effects on our children and will continue to look for ways to deal with this situation collectively.

## Collective action has shaped our community

Point St. Charles has a long history of community organizations engaged in finding solutions to problems of poor housing, lack of education, malnutrition and accessibility to medical care through community mobilization and political action. We thought back to some of the significant actions that have left an impact on us and have been the source of encouragement for ongoing involvement.

Twenty-five years ago some concerned citizens and medical students set up a mobile clinic[4] because of the lack of good medical care in the Point. It was very important for the community because it did not single out people as the needy poor, but was seen as a very supportive service that they were involved in. The Community Clinic grew out of this and became the first of its kind in Quebec. The C.L.S.C.'s (Centre Local de Services Communautaires — the system of government community clinics that have been set up throughout the province) were modelled after the Point clinic, but it remains as the only autonomous, community-run medical service. Last year when the government decided to incorporate it into the provincial system, the whole community rallied around to defend our right to maintain control. After a year with negotiations involving all the community groups and public meetings attended by hundreds of citizens, we won the right to remain autonomous. What a victory!

The Legal Clinic, which started in 1971 in much the same way as the Medical Clinic, was also a first for Quebec. Myrna recalled the help and support she received from the clinic when she went through a divorce 25 years ago. People really pulled together to guarantee that everyone would have the right to legal help regardless of whether they could afford to pay for it. There was a strong citizens' committee that has been very involved in running the clinic over the years. If people needed help with things they didn't understand and all the big words of legal documents or procedures, the Legal Clinic was always there for them. Even with all the cut-backs in legal aid services, our clinic has done their best to work the loop-holes and to bend the rules to be able to help the community.

A battle everyone remembers in the Point was the fight to keep the Fire Station as an historic site. It was to be demolished to make way for a highway to run right through the middle of the Point. The whole community defended the building, stopped the highway and now the Fire Station houses a Public Library and a Golden Age Centre. People really remember this as one of the big battles and a victory that has really made a difference in preserving the community.

The co-operative housing movement began in Point St. Charles over twenty years ago, through the Parallel Institute, a United Church funded project that was housed in St. Columba House. This developed into a housing movement that has succeeded in holding back a complete take-over of the community through gentrification and there are now approximately 40 percent of families in the Point in co-op housing. Point St. Charles is ideally located close to the core of downtown Montreal with easy access by public transit, making it a major target for "redevelopment." Without this mobilization, the community would never have been able to keep together and the effects of poverty would be even worse. Once again, with major funding sources disappearing for low-cost housing, it requires continued pressure and citizens' involvement to try to meet the heavy demands for such affordable housing.

As we spoke of the significance of these long-time struggles in our community, we appreciated how important this history has been in providing the base that has allowed this community to survive. The people have a tremendous pride in what has been built together and the hope for the future comes out of such shared experiences. It is a poor community, at times a tough community, but with a sense of spirit that is unique. What a gift!

# 3

# HOPE *in Action: The Experience of Three Community Groups*

$W$e are all involved in many activities and groups that are working to change living conditions in our community. To try to understand more fully what brings energy and hope through this engagement, we will look very specifically at the role of three different groups — the Point Adult Centre for Education (PACE), the Women's Discussion Group and the Point at Work co-operative (PAW). Our reflections are based on consultations with all the participants in these groups, followed by further discussion with our writing collective. The process itself has had significant effects and we will discuss these as well.

## The Point Adult Centre for Education (PACE)

Before PACE began in 1985, a lot of groundwork was done. It all began when the constant threat of closing Lorne School (the only English Protestant elementary school in the Point) affected its enrolment. A group of concerned women approached Faye Wakeling at St. Columba House, in hopes of getting assistance on how to deal with the Protestant School Board of Greater Montreal (P.S.B.G.M.) After numerous meetings together, we began our quest to seek out new ways of utilizing Lorne School.

We decided the best way to find out what the people wanted was to go out into the community. We conducted a door-to-door survey of Point St. Charles! A number of ideas were suggested, but the most popular one was an English Adult Education Centre situated right in our community.

After compiling our results, we met with representatives from the P.S.B.G.M. in an effort to convince them of the need for such a centre. We remember their initial reaction very well. They were no less than shocked that we would suggest such an idea. After all, there were already existing adult education centres at Westmount High School and at the High School of Montreal on University Street downtown. In their minds, these centres were easily accessible to citizens of Point St. Charles.

They had missed the importance of what we were trying to do. With 65 percent of the population on welfare or U.I.C. and 46.4 percent of citizens over fifteen who had not completed Grade 9 and with 55 percent of the population functionally illiterate, it was obvious that we needed a centre in our area that would be readily accessible and affordable. We needed to offer education that met the needs of people in the community who did not have good memories of school and courses that respected what they knew from their life experience. It wasn't a privilege. It was a right!

After many meetings with the Director of Adult Services and some of the commissioners, we finally received the mandate to go ahead. We also had succeeded in our request to have the appointment of a liaison person within the School Board to work with us. This proved to be a great asset in the coming months as it was crucial to have someone from "inside" the system, committed to supporting our struggle.

PACE officially began in the Fall of 1985, organized and run by women of the community. We were located on the third floor of Lorne School while the elementary school occupied the rest of the building. Although we had won the right to affordable English adult education in our own community, we knew there would be many obstacles to overcome. The only difference was that, with the help of Faye and St. Columba House, we had become more confident in what we could now do. We were making a difference!

## No typewriters, no typing

An example of the endless obstacles that we were forced to overcome concerned a typewriting class that we offered. We had sufficient registrants for this class, but we were told by the Director of Adult Services that we couldn't have the class because there weren't any typewriters available. This is where our liaison person came to the rescue. She found some manual typewriters for us to use in the class. We were then told we still couldn't have the class because we didn't have typing desks. Again, our liaison person came to the rescue, searched throughout the schools of the region and found some typing desks. Even though there were then objections from the school board that we should have electric typewriters, the class finally began. We did eventually get electric typewriters, but we never had any complaints from the students because the people of the Point were basically happy just to have the class. They were so easily pleased.

Our discouragement was starting to show. It seemed that every time we tried to get another course started, something came up, such as no sewing machines for the sewing course. Again, with the help of our liaison person, we managed to overcome these obstacles with the knowledge that there were more hurdles to come. Even though there were times we felt like giving up, we knew that we *never* would. We also had so much support from other community organizations and churches, not only to help keep Lorne School open, but also to keep PACE going. They believed in us and this only helped us to fight that much harder.

Although our fight to keep Lorne School open ended in defeat three years later, we knew the battle had just begun. We weren't going to lose PACE too. We had put so much time and energy into PACE and we were finally becoming a symbol of hope in desperate times. There was no way we were going to lose that hope without a fight. Our educational goals must be allowed to develop and PACE would remain open.

## Elementary school closes

Lorne School closed in the summer of 1987 and was bought by the City of Montreal that same summer. Again, after a lot of mobilization and pressure, we signed a lease with the City of Montreal from October 1987 to June 1988 to use the school building. Two years were spent in the abandoned school. We incurred considerable expenses for tenant's and personal liability insurance, as well as maintenance and cleaning costs. The P.S.B.G.M. would only fund courses that were eligible for subsidization through the Quebec Ministry of Education, but there were other course needs that couldn't be met because of particular restrictions or tuition expenses that the low-income population that we serve couldn't meet. The P.S.B.G.M. would only provide funding if we could get a rent-free locale and they provided partial funding for a co-ordinator.

It wasn't an easy task maintaining PACE in an abandoned building. Some nights when the heating system broke down, it was so cold during the classes that we had to wear our winter coats and boots to stay warm. This didn't seem to deter our students. We continued PACE for three more years (1987-1990) in the abandoned Lorne School building.

We had over 200 registrations each semester. This widespread interest and enthusiasm for learning reinforced our conviction of the need to continue to offer adult education to the anglophone sector that had no such centre before PACE started.

The City of Montreal also realized the need for PACE. They not only allowed us to stay, finally rent-free, in Lorne School, they also helped us to move to an alternate school building to continue our programs while they had the Lorne building renovated. With the support of the City of Montreal behind us, we were able to negotiate with the Catholic School Commission to use the top floor of Jeanne Leber School (the French Catholic elementary school) from the Fall of 1990 to the Spring of 1991. The City of Montreal moved our equipment that we needed to the new location and stored the rest for us.

Lorne School was turned into co-operative housing, but one floor was set aside for PACE. Before renovations began on Lorne School, representatives from the City met with us to see what our needs for PACE were and asked for our input on the number of classrooms we needed, the location of washrooms, design of a kitchen/sewing room, outlets, and so on. The City of Montreal understood our conviction for the need of English Adult Education in the community. What a breakthrough! With the stability of having a permanent locale we began concentrating on the actual running of PACE and offering the courses that the people wanted. PACE was finally making its mark in the community.

## Criteria changes

Even when the Ministry of Education changed its criteria for funding and we found ourselves slipping between the cracks, we stood up for what we had already achieved. Just before our Fall 1991 session was to begin, we received news from the P.S.B.G.M. that all our teachers' salary funding of $25,000 had been cut. It felt like we were starting the fight all over again. This time, through St. Columba House, many United Church people got involved and organized a telephone blitz to the Chairman of the School

Board. When presidents of major companies voiced their concerns, the Board had to respond to their pressure. The P.S.B.G.M. found the money from another budget to allow PACE to continue.

When we moved back into our newly renovated locale in the Fall of 1991, we had a sense of pride in knowing that we would finally be allowed to pursue our educational goals. Those who had been a part of PACE from the beginning found their dream was now a reality.

We now had a permanent locale and funding for academic courses. The P.S.B.G.M. granted some funding for our co-ordinator, for teachers' salaries and materials for academic courses such as French, Computer (Basic, Lotus, Word Perfect), Spanish, New Math, English as a Second Language, and so on. Each year we submit an Annual Report of our activities to the P.S.B.G.M. Adult Education Committee and request a grant for the upcoming year. Finally it seems that they have recognized the importance of this work and have been very supportive. Their funding is very important, but we, the community, must maintain control over the education in the centre.

PACE pays for the teachers' salaries and materials for leisure courses from money collected at registration and other grants or donations we have received.[5] Over the years some of the leisure courses we have offered are Sewing, Arts and Crafts, Aerobics, Cooking, Calligraphy, Silkscreening, Jazz Ballet, Drawing and Painting, Self-Defense for Women, Tai-Chi, Hairdressing, C.P.R. and First Aid. These courses are usually taught by people in the community who have special talents and this is an important way for us to help people use their skills. We also find funding for the literacy courses that are so vital. However, we have had great difficulty encouraging those who do not read to participate in classes. The literacy classes have been so significant for those who have attended but we are not satisfied with the number of people we have reached.

This year we had a membership drive to help build up our grassroots support system. Members of PACE receive reduced course rates and a voice in the running of the centre. The only criteria for becoming a member of PACE is that you must reside in Point St. Charles and support our goals.

It has been a long, difficult struggle to begin the centre and to keep PACE open, but the outcome has been very rewarding. We are fulfilling a need in our community and at the same time we are helping people to realize their potential and capabilities. We have become a stepping stone to further education for some people. For others, we are the place to come and learn very informally.

PACE is truly education with a difference! Citizens have been involved with setting up and developing the centre and providing a strong back-up network for PACE.[6]

## The Impact of PACE

The PACE Committee gathered to look back over the years of involvement in fighting for and building this centre and to discuss what impact it has had on our community. We felt that one of the most important achievements of PACE has been that the students feel better about themselves and have developed a sense of pride in their ability to learn. A lot of people say that when they first come to take a course, it is primarily because it is cheap. But then when they get into it, many are very surprised at what they have learned and that they are able to learn. They didn't realize what potential they had.

We recalled a very special story from our first year at PACE during the year-end evaluation meeting with all the participants. Someone pointed out that Elizabeth was scrubbing the floors and doing the cleaning all by herself, that this wasn't fair and the group would have to do something about it. An older woman stood up very straight and with great pride said; "Well! I learned how to use a computer this year. If I can use a computer, I can do anything! So I certainly can mop the floor and set things up here." It was the way she said it that was so unforgettable — *"if I can learn to use the computer, I can do anything!"* It was like something had opened up for her.

Elizabeth smiled and said; "This is what we wanted. This is part of the impact we had hoped for. It can be so intimidating to go to a big college or a school outside of the community, but we have bypassed all of that. People say that it is very informal and friendly. People are really happy to be a part of it. I have had such good feedback. They know that they are welcome to share their ideas. It is not just going in and following a curriculum from the teacher. They are actually a part of what they are going to learn and that is the difference. That is our main success right there."

One member replied; "People who work in PACE are from this community. So it began right here and it is going to stay here."

Donna agreed enthusiastically and said; "It was just the common people who started it. We had no experience in running an adult education centre or formal education or popular education." We learned though as we went along and we also made mistakes.

Faye added; "And you didn't give up, which surprised the School Board. I think that in itself has had an impact and given hope to the community. You have hung in there and carried on in spite of enormous obstacles all these years."

Elizabeth responded; "There is a lot of hope and people *do* see the hope. We struggled for a long time and there were so many people behind us. You always think that if you are running an adult centre you are supposed to be a university graduate. But we are not and we are proud that we are not. We started this out of a need and it is still here now. PACE is here to stay. We are a thorn in some people's side, like the School Board, but they will just have to get used to us, I guess."

One member of the committee spoke of becoming more confident since she has been involved in PACE and helping with the literacy class. This work has brought out her own skills and a new understanding of what she can do in the future. Another young woman found that her "people skills" were put to the test and she has learned that she is very good at encouraging people to talk. Others pointed out how she keeps everyone laughing and spirits high.

There are people from the community that have taught courses that had never done this before and were surprised to find that they could teach others (such as ceramics, aerobics, carpentry, sewing, drawing, cooking, hairdressing). This has had an important impact on the community.

There are lots of challenges ahead and goals that we have not yet met. We have been able to reach very few of the 50 percent of our community that needs literacy help and we need to utilize popular education methods in more of our courses. Many parents need child care to take classes and that is a goal for the future. We renewed our determination to bring more people into the committee work so that they could both help find solutions and also reap the benefits each of us have found in our involvement with the centre. PACE is an example that you *can* fight bureaucracy and win. It shows there is room for everyone's skills and that even a community like ours can succeed in education.

# The Women's Discussion Group

"We are a support group. When we come together we realize we all have the same problems really and we are not isolated. We may not have solutions, but just to know that other women are in the same boat, makes a big difference in how you feel about your situation. When you talk about something you don't feel so alone."

This was the first response when the group discussed why we gathered. For more than ten years the group has met once a week at St. Columba House and during that time there has been remarkable growth, challenge and results. We agreed to participate in this reflection for the women's collective writing, with the understanding that we would not be necessarily identified and that we all would have some say in the final write-up. So this discussion became a way for the whole group to reflect on what we have been about over the years.

We realize that our expectations vary and also that at different stages in our lives we are looking for different types of involvement. For some, just to get out and have adult company is a marvellous treat. "As a single parent, it is important to get together and also to have a break from my son. When you have kids, you just don't have an opportunity to sit around and talk because you are worrying about the baby crying or something. But here, we have no worries because someone is looking after the kids." For many women this is the first motivation that brings them into the group, but after that what keeps us involved are the activities, the discussions and really getting into issues that concern us as women.

## Getting out and trying new things

We began to talk about what has changed us over the years and for many of us the outings we have gone on together have really been highlights. A few times a year we receive subsidized tickets from the Centaur Theatre and we have seen some wonderful plays. For many of us this was a first and something we would never have been able to do on our own. We recalled the play we had seen by a playwright from the Point who writes about our community. One of the women said, "I remember going to David Fennario's play and we weren't happy with how he showed the Point. So we called him here to talk with the Women's Group about it. He came with his "bodyguard," as he called him, to talk to us. There were about eighteen women there. It was really neat that we could actually do that.

"I always grew up thinking that the rules were like this and that's the way it goes. But now, with other actions we have taken and calling in David Fennario, it is teaching me that, Hey, if you don't like it, you have the right to stand up and say something. No matter who it is against, even if it is an authority figure, that as an individual or as a group you have that right. You don't have to sit back and say that's the rules or that's the way it goes and we're not allowed to say anything about it. I can stand up for my rights now."

"For me, Centaur Theatre just seemed out of my reach before I came to the Women's Group. I don't know if I thought that I didn't belong there, but it was out of my reach. So when we started going, the first time I went I just couldn't believe I was going. Then after we went it was the issues that were important. The play always represented something and when we came back we always had an important issue to talk about after. If we liked it or didn't like it, there were still important issues. In some way, either in our community or in our own lives, we could find something in it. It really, really made a big change."

"The Arena art show by local artists that we went to a few weeks ago was very interesting. I wouldn't have gone on my own. I didn't even know about it. It's like we live here but we don't really know what is out there. When we start going out to places in Montreal, we realize what we're missing."

Our visit to the Montreal Museum of Fine Arts to see the Duane Hansen exhibit was very powerful. His sculptures of real life figures, many of them working class people, had been very disturbing to see. A little girl, sitting alone in a corner, looking so vulnerable, was a hard reminder of bad memories for many. We found it tough, depressing and very moving as we felt the despair and isolation of all the figures. As one woman said, "That's how it is these days. You work like a dog and what do you get out of it?" In our discussion we recalled how much this exhibit was like real life and that it was good to see such reality displayed in a large museum. Someone remarked that "it showed the well-to-do people as well and you could see that money isn't everything. Even if you were rich, it showed the worries and the struggles. It was sad. It showed life like it is. We have problems here, but there are a lot of things we have here, like getting together as a community, that they don't have." Another commented that "It showed in a sense that life is what we make of it. Not that it has to be sad. There is a lot of suffering and struggle and we have to go through that. But it showed that if you want to have a good life, a happy life — whatever happy is — we have to work at it. All those figures in the exhibit looked so alone. Even the group of construction workers having lunch paid no attention to each other. There wasn't any sense of community there at all. That was what was so shocking!"

Another very important experience that has left its mark on us, was attending the performance of Beethoven's Ninth Symphony. This was a first for many of us and full of the unexpected. "I was really surprised. I expected a man to be conducting, but when I got there it was a woman and she was wonderful! You could see every facial expression from where we sat. She was very soft and every gesture was soft. It was a pleasure for her to do that. It was her job I guarantee, but it was more than a job. It was life-giving. She gave." Somehow to watch this woman did something extraordinary to us. She was so encouraging! It was just like she was dancing.

One of the women said, "I remember when we were asked if we wanted to go, I kept saying 'It's not my thing.' But I think it was more of a fear that I was nervous that I wouldn't appreciate the music because it wasn't what I was brought up with. I didn't have an appreciation of classical music. This seems to be more of a middle class family experience. I was more worried about not fitting in than I actually was about enjoying the music." That is part of what is behind the trips we take as a Women's Group. Some of these things cost money but some of them don't (like the symphony that night) and it encourages us to go again. On the way home one of the women said that for awhile she really concentrated hard on the music and then she couldn't keep it up. So she sat back and just let it "wash over her." It was such a wonderful expression. It meant so much to her. As a single parent with two children and a new baby, she had been finding life very hard. The symphony calmed her and for a short time, she could let things go. Others had also been surprised to find that in the midst of the turmoil they were in, this was a way to let things go. It was as though in these moments there was a way to get in touch with some inner calmness and peace.

## Women under pressure

A very important part of our work together is looking at particular concerns of women, learning more about ourselves and why women are under such pressure in our society, educating ourselves and the community, and taking actions. We have had many sessions on violence against women that have been both heavy and helpful.

We talked about why we think the violence happens and have looked at the effects of T.V., newspapers and advertising. We have seen what a powerful effect this has on encouraging violence against women and bad images of women. We have talked with women who work in women's shelters to understand the new stalking law and to look more closely at why it is so hard for women to get out of abusive situations. We invited the local police to come to our group to discuss how they deal with domestic violence and to share our concerns about inadequate protection for women. It has helped us to understand how big the job is and that we have to work at solutions together.

We have looked for ways to broaden the understanding in the community about the causes of the increasing violence against women through animating discussions in the Community Lunch program where families, men and women, gather weekly. Each year we have had a memorial service of the Montreal Massacre and this past year on December 6th, the Women's Group planned a remembrance for this gathering. Candles were extinguished with the naming of the fourteen women victims followed by an invitation for people to come forward to extinguish other candles in memory of women friends or relatives who were victims. It was a very profound and moving event, with men choosing to come forward as well. It ended with us all going outside to release 125 white helium balloons with messages of hope for a better, safer world for women and our children. The Women's Group has taken a leadership role in the community that is beginning to have very important effects on ourselves and others.

## Standing against abuse

Many of the women were involved in the action we took to support a woman who had been sexually abused by a doctor in a local clinic. Louise had talked to Faye about her experience and then had agreed to share it with the rest of the group in the hopes that we could help her to deal with it. Many of us have been victims of abuse, but this situation had a more public dimension about it. We shared other experiences, our powerlessness as poor women when dealing with the medical profession, and also our fears, that as mothers of young girls, this could also happen to our daughters. We decided to act! So Louise made an appointment with the clinic director without saying that she would be coming with friends. Six women gathered that morning, some with babies in carriages, to accompany her as support. We walked through the streets with a determination that was so evident that people we passed by asked us what we were up to. It was a difficult encounter that left us shaking after a very volatile discussion with the male director who insisted that Louise had "misunderstood." Nevertheless, we left knowing that we had won something important. We had moved from the shame and anger of the first discussion to the place where, together, we had been able to stand up and name the abuser. We had taken charge and been empowered by our action.

This has remained a powerful memory of collective action that has had effects even beyond our group. The story has been told widely in the community and is one of those touchstone experiences that help us to find courage to act in other situations.

*Messages of hope for a safer world for women.*

# Women Against Contamination (WAC)

We have frequently discussed the very high incidence of allergies, asthma, respiratory problems and learning disabilities of children in our community and the fact that studies indicate these are much more serious than in other neighbourhoods. We are also very concerned by the reports of 40 properties in the Point that have been identified as having dangerous levels of soil pollution when testing was done prior to new construction. Half of these properties have been decontaminated, but there has been no testing of the ground around the homes beside these contaminated areas or in the rest of the community. The City of Montreal discovered that one of the playgrounds is on contaminated land and their solution was just to remove the sandbox from the park. The Lachine Canal that runs along the Point has been the object of studies that have cost millions of dollars, as the Federal Government has explored possible ways to decontaminate these waters so that the area could be used as a recreation canal for outsiders.

In 1993, after months of discussion about the possible connection between illness and pollution, the Women's Group decided to form a sub-committee, the Women Against Contamination (WAC) to study this problem. In spite of all the fears of what we might find, we *had* to know the truth. It was a big decision to make. Since then we have been learning together to do research on contamination and to interpret studies that have been done. At one time the Point was the most highly industrialized area in Canada and for more than a century, factories have dumped their waste directly into the ground and, by way of underground rivers, into the Lachine Canal. In all the studies that have been done, no one has bothered to look at the health affects of this contamination on the people in our community. We have run up against brick walls frequently as the different levels of government have made it clear that they feel we have no right to see the results of their testing. It is like opening a can of worms that no one wants us to look into.

We convinced the local community clinic of the importance of our concerns and they are now working with us. An epidemiologist from McGill is helping us learn about contaminants and testing procedures that can be used. We have developed a project to start testing our children for the presence of lead, mercury, arsenic, cadmium, and other contaminents. A very crucial aspect of this work is the committee's determination to learn all they can about the problem and be included in every step of the study and research. We have delved into areas we are completely ignorant about and have been so grateful for the patient support of some experts in the field that are helping us to understand. Taking on this responsibility has increased our confidence in ourselves and our determination that the lives of people in our community be respected.

In addition, we have found a heightened awareness in the community of environmental concerns. We are all talking of articles on contamination in the newspapers, studies done on the regional high school that was just closed because of unhealthy air, old dumping sites people remember and new information on asthma and allergies. It is like the stone in the pool that has sent out ripples throughout the community.

As one woman said, "I think that people thought that when we started to talk about WAC it was just one of our whims and maybe we would just talk about it, but that was as far as it would go. But it has really got off the ground and everybody thinks that it is very important. We are really going to do something."

## We are about change

A lot is happening in our Women' Group, but we also have some frustrations about not accomplishing all that we would like to do.

We feel that there are many more women that we should be reaching through our activities because there are such high needs in the community. We have also found that if a woman finds a job, she loses the support of the group. We have started a group in the evenings once a month, but it is not enough and the women don't really feel a part of the group. We had also hoped that responsibility for our sessions would be more shared than it is, but that is a goal that Myrna and Faye (the animators) have had to let go. For many of us, there are too many pressures already to take on another responsibility in the group. Free space is often what is needed most and we understand that. However, for special events, such as animation on topics in the Community Lunch program, there has been a wonderful sharing and participation. On these occasions some women surprise themselves with unexpected gifts as speakers and leaders.

We are a group that is about change — change in ourselves, in relationships within our families and for women in the community. When we

*Following a lively skit (a dialogue between a baby girl and a baby boy) Christine leads an animated discussion about gender roles at the Community Lunch program.*

talked about how we ourselves had changed through the group, there were some wonderful stories of new life and often courageous new steps.

One woman who shared her story, spoke of how it had been so difficult for her to go out of the house. With the help of the group she had been able to share many of her problems, find new ways to be involved as a volunteer in the community, participated in the Worship Group and eventually took responsibility for the Collective Kitchens. She discovered new skills and ways to share them with others. She said; "For me, the group brought me out because I never went out before. Now I am out instead of being home all the time. That is what the group has done for me."

Another woman spoke up and said; "I think the big thing for me through the group was to find out that it was alright for me to need help and to seek out professional help for my problems. I would never have gone otherwise. But the group used to say that it is okay to get help and there is nothing wrong with that. It has been almost a year now that I have been going to a counsellor and it took many years to get to that place. I don't know if I ever would have gone on my own. I would like to think I would have, but I doubt it very much. I was always worried about it being a put-down, but the group never saw it as that and have been very supportive with me. It was a big thing that I took that step."

"I would not let anybody look after my baby before. But now, coming here I have found out that it is alright to leave my children with someone. Now I am able to do that. They are still upset when I leave, but it has been good for us."

## Changes within our community

When we talked about what affect the group had on the community, someone piped in, "Let's talk about our partners!" That got a real good laugh and then we started to look at what changes there had been. One woman said that "Before coming here I had the kids and I had my husband. (Great gales of laughter!) I was always known as his wife or their mother and I didn't know who I was. Now I know and even though I am still learning, I realize that I have my own identity. Now I make my own decisions about things that are going on in my life. Just because I have a husband doesn't necessarily mean I can't do my own things too. But for my husband it was 'Not that Women's Group again!' He used to encourage me to make my own decisions but when I started doing it he had mixed feelings. He was so used to me being one way, and then he saw me starting to change." There were a few partners who were quite angry with the group and really let us know it. It wasn't always easy for some women to participate.

We raised the question about what effect the group has had, on the community and named some of the small changes we had brought about. Although we have animated some very important discussions in community groups about roles of women, violence against women, the effect of the Social Reform Policy on women, worked with francophone women's groups to develop working goals, and participated in community actions, we did not feel we had accomplished enough. We were very confident of the effect on ourselves, our families and children, but the larger community seemed to be hard to measure.

Our celebration each year of International Women's Day on March 8th has been a very important time to look at the struggles and goals of women in the Point. There have been about 100 women from the community and sometimes women invited from nearby Kahnawake (an Aboriginal reserve) and anti-poverty groups. We have shared food together and spoken of all the battles women have won over the years and in many different countries. Our theme one year was "Women on the Move" and we were encouraged, energized and even more ready to hang in after listening to women's stories and seeing how far we had come.

## The "bent-over woman"

Over the years we have so often spoken of the story of Jesus healing the "bent-over woman" as we have discussed the struggles of women in our community. In the light of our writing about the actions and struggle of women, we decided to turn once again to this passage:

> One Sabbath Jesus was teaching in a synagogue. A woman there had an evil spirit that had kept her sick for eighteen years: she was bent over and could not straighten up at all. When Jesus saw her, he called out to her, "Woman, you are free from your sickness" He placed his hands on her, and at once she straightened herself up and praised God.   — Luke 13:10-13

Donna commented that "the first thing I noticed was that Jesus called her. Usually it was people going to Jesus and asking for healing, but this time he actually called her out, even though she didn't ask for it. She had carried this burden for so long and as I think of the Women's Discussion group, I was thinking about how it takes some women so long to work through or try to bring about changes at home. It took me a few years of going to the group before I could actually find the confidence to stand up and say 'I have a life too and I can do what I want too! I can make my own decisions too. But it took a while to change my attitudes and my way of thinking, and to build confidence. It is not something that comes overnight."

Myrna added that "it takes the support of other women to help you to know that it is alright to stand up for what you really believe in."

Faye commented that "It is so often someone else that says something that connects with what we are dealing with. In that sense it is like in this passage where Jesus calls out to the woman. I think that happens a lot in the Women's Discussion group. There are women that do not necessarily come because they want to get stronger, but maybe just to get out of the house. But then sometimes people's comments will help them change."

We spoke of ways in which people have called each other out and that for us, those words "woman you are free from your illness" were like someone saying "yes, you can do it."

Elizabeth responded; "It is like we were the bent-over women over all those years and all of a sudden — but it wasn't really all of a sudden — you finally get there."

Myrna said; "I don't think we realize ourselves all the changes that have happened, because it is such a long struggle. Sometimes we don't see it for ourselves unless someone points it out. I know it is a crazy thing to use, but it is like you finally see the light. You don't see it and then all of a sudden it makes sense and things fall into place. There is still going to be continuous struggle and hard work, but you are not all the way back where you were. You know that you have to keep going."

When we talked about the devastating response of the synagogue leaders to the healing of the bent over woman, we wondered why they were so upset about what happened and what they had to lose:

> The official of the synagogue was angry that Jesus had healed on the Sabbath, so he spoke up and said to the people, "There are six days in which we should work; so come during those days and be healed, but not on the Sabbath!" The Lord answered him, "You hypocrites! Any one of you would untie his ox or donkey from the stall and take it out to give it water on the Sabbath. Now here is this descendant of Abraham whom Satan has kept bound up for eighteen years; should she not be released on the Sabbath?" His answer made his enemies ashamed of themselves, while the people rejoiced over all the wonderful things that he did. — Luke 13:14-17

Donna connected the resistance of this leader to discussions in the Women's Group about how women are afraid to rock the boat. "Because if one person changes, everyone else has to change along with it. What I do, affects my family. So for the officials around this woman, it was like Jesus had rocked the boat and they wanted an excuse to have something against Jesus again."

Melissa said; "It is like the people are trying to control the situation because she was standing up for herself. She was getting strength and they did not approve of that. She was also getting attention, so they were trying to put her back in her place. It is like the Women's Group and the put-downs we get for going to it."

We thought about the women who were accused of being lesbians because they came to the group. The men who said that to the women didn't really believe it, but used it as a threat because *they* were feeling threatened. A lot of men like to control their women and women's groups challenge this. Changes that start in such groups are carried into their homes too.

Faye commented; "I found the words *'bound up'* very hard. It is an awful phrase. It doesn't sound as though it is just by chance, but that something has been done and she has been bound up."

"I think she was a hooker," Melissa said. "It is like the bounding you would have from your pimp, but when you are freed then it is like you are really free. It is not like she was hurt or had sickness. In those days the biggest sin you could have was being an adulteress or a hooker. She didn't lead the right life in their eyes. I took the "bent over" as meaning being pressured by life. It sounded to me that the devil controls her spirit, but it is not the devil that makes you sick. Life makes you sick. I can relate to this passage pressure-wise. Being poverty-stricken is pressure enough."

Myrna felt that there was so much in this passage and she didn't see it as "a miracle passage in the sense of Jesus saying 'woman you are free' and all of a sudden she is healed. I don't know what this bent-over woman looked like, but I think it was the burden and the heavy weight of everyday life. When Jesus said that she would be free it doesn't mean that she would be just carefree. The struggle would continue because she would have to go on living with whatever that burden was."

That is what it is like in our community and Elizabeth said; "It is like the bent-over woman was lowered. It is like people here in our community who are put in a lower category. The freedom comes in helping each other to stand up straight."

# Point At Work (PAW)

*I think the fact that we have come this far and have put in
so much of our time and energy and ourselves, is what keeps
me going. We have all given a part of our life together and I
could not come to the place where I would say it is over. But
I am not saying it is not frustrating not having a pay and
not yet seeing our goals being fulfilled. — Melissa*

The upholstery project, Point At Work (PAW), is in serious financial difficulty and the group is trying to assess what the next step will be. We offer our reflections on what it is like to develop a vision of fair work, to seek to create and offer something of lasting value to our community, to be determined to find a way to create employment in the face of increasing joblessness, and to find that we are not succeeding.

The idea for PAW came out of the Women's Discussion Group as we spoke of our vision of a better community. We spent a whole session talking about a factory that would produce something of value for the Point, would provide work that brought dignity, paid decent wages and allowed the workers to share responsibility while learning together. We wanted it to go further than just wishful thinking and the Staff of St. Columba House took the decision to make it a priority to start a work collective. The 26 week government Job Development Projects that went nowhere had been very discouraging and we were determined to create employment through a worker's co-operative.

Unemployed people in the community, interested in a job creation project, began to meet together to discuss possibilities. The "Rent-a-Hand" job bank was started and others looked at the feasibility of a work co-op such as upholstery, minor electrical repairs, woodworking, transportation or home repairs. After many months of research, the decision was made to begin the reupholstery project that we hoped would provide training in a trade, create jobs and help those on low-income have good-looking furniture, subsidizing work for them through outside contracts. Although there were men involved in the original committee, they did not choose to stay on when the PAW project began in the fall of 1989.

## Sharing tools

Six women started the co-operative and we committed ourselves to a certain number of volunteer hours each month to learn the trade. We hired a teacher and paid her with any profits from our work. The first year was a real challenge, since we put in a lot of time and often received no pay. Sharing one set of tools between six women was an experience! Learning to accept each others' strengths and weaknesses was enlightening but also frustrating. But we were learning, transforming furniture that was sometimes brought in off the streets and taking responsibility for the management of our own co-op. We sought out donations of material from fabric companies, received donations of tools and a great second-hand industrial sewing machine from the company where our instructor worked.

The goals for our co-operative were, first, to provide stable employment, second, to do something that was creative and of value, and third, to provide a service to our community that would particularly help those who had very little money.

*Melissa and Shirley hard at work bringing new life to old furniture.*

Six years later, four of the six founding women were still working in the co-operative. When we looked back at what motivated us to get involved originally, we were surprised to find how different our expectations had been. For both Barbara and Shirley, the motivation was to learn how to do upholstery as a trade, but they were not counting on it for a permanent job.

Donna had been on the original planning committee and recalled; "I got involved because I thought it sounded really neat, something new and different. Upholstery seemed the logical choice. I was looking for a job and something to do with your hands really interested me."

Melissa recalls that she had applied for a job in "Working Out," a 26 week Job Development Project at St. Columba House, and was asked if she got the job would she be willing to help to co-ordinate the new upholstery project. In her usual frank, direct way, Melissa said; "So what was I going to say? — No? Of course I didn't. That was in September before it got off the ground, but everything was already formed as to how it was going to start. That is how I got involved. I had to be willing to work in upholstery if I took the 'Working Out' job. Of course I said yes. It was like you had no choice. It is never a project I would have chosen. There are too many other needs in the community such as clothing or a food co-operative that I would have chosen over upholstery. Even though it was a goal to help the poor people in the area, it was still too expensive for them. My friend Louina, who has been our instructor, was an upholsterer then and I knew how expensive the work was. I didn't understand how we could lower the prices enough for people here. But after I was in it, I enjoyed the co-operative and really wanted to see it get off the ground. By that time I was in it for my own self and the job aspect was very important."

Sandra and Diane started because they wanted jobs. They enjoyed learning upholstery but it was more for the employment. Both of them had to leave the co-operative after three years, because of PAW's financial instability. Often paycheques would be weeks late because there wasn't sufficient revenue after all the bills were paid and their families could no longer survive without a more steady income. It was a real blow to lose them!

# Managing the business

We have gone through many stages during our short history, from our volunteer year at the beginning, to receiving federal funding to pay salaries and a full-time teacher for eight months. We have used job training funds to learn about co-op development, business management, wood refinishing and even had an ergonomist who worked with us to ensure that we were not abusing our bodies through bad work habits or conditions. From the beginning we have been committed to helping each person learn all aspects of the business instead of dividing up the tasks. Maybe it wasn't realistic to think that everybody should learn everything and we should have specialized a bit earlier. We have all been laid off at one time or another but have continued to work as volunteers during these periods to keep the co-op going. We have given a lot of ourselves.

When we received the government funding, we had to make a crucial decision, whether we would hire a project manager to train us in the business aspects or an upholstery teacher to learn the trade. We opted for the upholstery teacher, because this is a profession that takes so long to learn. We learned all aspects of the trade, stripping furniture down to the base and building it back up with springs, stuffing and covering. This was great for developing our skills, but we had serious lacks in the business management side of the co-op. We are really paying for this now. We were all so keen on becoming better upholsterers and none of us wanted to take on the management of the project.

Melissa has recently taken on the responsibility of co-ordinator and has received extra training in business management. But that was not an easy decision. Melissa says that she "didn't want to take on being manager at first. I was reluctant to take on the work because we all know each other very well and I didn't want to be hassled. I never take myself as being in charge though. I should have been doing the management a lot earlier and the work with a business consultant is really helping us."

The question "If we had it to do over again...?" brought out a lot of suggestions. Some felt that we would have done better if we had started with the planning and business training early on so that when we got into the upholstery work we would understand what we were up against. Others said that if that is how it was started, they probably would never have got involved or stuck it out. They wanted to learn a trade and produce work as soon as possible. However, if we were advising another co-operative, we would suggest that it would be beneficial to take the time to see how other similar businesses work and learn from them.

We feel that the way we approached the project may have been due to us being women. Without prior experience in business, it would have been hard for us to believe we could start off on our own. We all said that even though we may have dreamed of it, we would have been afraid to take the steps to start our own business. Instead we chose to get into the actual upholstery work, get really involved in it and then work to make it a long-term job.

We looked at the fact that what we did is very common for women. We were asked to come in, learn something and volunteer some time. How many times do women do this? Interestingly enough, the men in the original group were not willing to do that. They wanted to see a job tomorrow or to be more assured that as a business it was going to work.

We still all agreed that to start a co-op you would have to be willing to put in a lot of volunteer time. However, now we would start differently. We realize that if it is necessary to take extra courses, it would have to be in the evening on our own time. We would leave production-line time for production. We have always been very supportive of each other being involved in other important activities in the building, taking time off for our children when necessary and participating in community meetings that dealt with more than the running of the co-op. This has been very important for us all, but it certainly doesn't help a business make it.

## Our goals are hard to reach

The biggest disappointment has been the inability to continue to offer reupholstery to people in the community who have little money and this has been a hard, ongoing discussion.

Melissa said; "That was one of the things that kept me going with reupholstery. We were going to reach the poor — people that really needed it. That was what kept me on and now, that is not what is happening. We have known we haven't been able to do this for the last couple of years. There are people here who really could use the furniture, but there is no way we will ever be able to reach them, unless we could do it for nothing. These are people that get their furniture out of the alleys. There are many, many families in the Point that need our service but could never pay even our "fixed-income" price for it. We have helped some fire victims and we use donated material to keep the price as low as possible for those on welfare and low incomes, but I just feel that our upholstery project cannot help the poor. We reach people on low incomes, to redo kitchen chairs, et cetera — but not the poor."

Elizabeth tried to be encouraging and said; "I know that is not your main goal, but maybe it is a start."

"But we are getting further away from our goal though," Melissa replied. Before we used to do work at very low prices and take the losses. I argued with the instructor in the Business Course that we didn't want to charge $20 an hour to cover salaries and expenses. He said that it wouldn't work, but I said it was important for us to offer it at a price people could pay. But then we realized that we can't make a living like this. So we started raising prices. It seems like we are getting further and further away from our goal, not getting closer. I need a job and the money is important. But to feel good about myself I want more than a job and more than a salary. I want to be able to do something for people. That has always been important for me. Not that I have a lot better than them, but I have more than a lot of people."

We began to point out how much the workers in the co-operative had learned, the beautiful furniture they produce and the fact that their co-operative has really been important to the community as an example of self-employment. Myrna went on to say how sad she has felt about the difficulties they have been having "after all the hard work, the time and all the effort that people put into it. You have worked very hard. I am sad that there are aspects of it that you are unhappy with, but like everything else, maybe something will happen that will give you inspiration."

Melissa shared her frustration, but was determined to deal with the reality they faced as she pointed out that "it takes more than just wanting it to work. I think we need to get stabilized as a company. We are just realizing that now. As a company we have to have stable employment and that should have been our first goal. Then we would be able to offer services to very low-income people. For the last few years we have been trying to do both — the employment and making the business good, as well as offering our services. I think we have to be stable before we can do that and that is what is hard to face."

Faye mentioned other factors that are producing problems for the co-operative and said; "Donna, you talked about your daughter's economics class example of a guy who was trying to make a business profitable by cutting back workers. What you have also been trying to do is to be fair and supportive to each other in a co-operative. You have been respecting people's gifts and their lack of gifts, as well as not making a profit from people who can't afford it. What you are up against is a business world that is set up differently. So I think that this does not mean that you give up all your goals, but don't blame yourself for your failure to reach them all. That doesn't mean that just feeling good about having ideals is going to put bread on the table or make the business work. What you are up against is a world in which the labour market can charge lower wages than people can live on, concentrate on high production and lay somebody off with no notice if they find they are not productive enough."

We agreed that the time had come to consolidate the business, to not let go of our goal to serve the community, but to see that as a longer term objective. We were reminded that the same thing happened to PACE whose goal was to do more challenging popular education work from the beginning. At the start, with all the struggle to keep it alive, that goal had to be put on hold. Now, eight years later, the time has come to start getting into the kind of education PACE wanted to do from the beginning.

## Learning, growing and changing

Throughout the years of working together, we have seen changes in each other as a result of the PAW project. We all are very proud of the furniture we transform and know from happy customers that we really have developed our creative skills. But beyond that, our work has had other effects on us and how we feel about ourselves. To be able to speak so straightforwardly about our own feelings and progress was a major step in itself.

When we asked what changes we had experienced, we were pleasantly surprised that Shirley spoke up right away to say; "Sometimes I am a little quiet, but I speak up more now. Before I was so quiet and kept my feelings inside all the time. I never like to hurt people's feeling, but I have learned to speak up. But sometimes I think I am a bit hard now." We assured Shirley how much better it is for everyone now that she says what is on her mind. She is more independent than she was and takes more chances on her own.

Melissa, in her direct, assertive way said; "I'm stronger, much stronger in speaking my mind. Believe it or not I don't always speak my mind. Just standing up for myself — my rights, my own personal respect for myself, I have changed a lot. I don't take B.S. from a lot of people I would have taken it from before. I feel more important now because I am able to make decisions. My job downstairs (PAW is located in the basement of St. Columba House) has played a major role in that. I think of my job as having control, not over people, but over what is happening. I feel responsible for myself and my own actions. It has changed me a lot. There are things I'll always carry with me from what I have learned downstairs, but I'd like to see myself progress to something else."

Donna very quietly replied; "I am slowly learning to be independent. I feel as a person I am stronger, in the sense that I feel I am capable of doing things now. I may not be as hesitant to try something new, even though new things still scare me. I have learned a lot about my community and find that I am into a lot more now. With the women downstairs, we are learning to get along and learning how to cope with each other's differences. It is also not being afraid to take some chances — safe chances."

Barbara did not really see changes in herself and feels that she has always been able to be very straightforward. But Melissa expressed concern that Barbara had changed. "I love Barbara, but I find her tired now. She comes in tired and it takes everything out of her now. You have had a lot of things happen to you in the last year and that doesn't help. You haven't had time to rest." Barbara agreed with what was said, thought about it over the following weeks and she made an important decision to cut back on her work with PAW.

In spite of all the hard work, the weeks without pay and the constant pressure of whether we will be able to carry on, we have learned and grown together. We have created jobs for ourselves and we are in control of our business. As Melissa said, "Where else could you work for eight hours a day and have the fun we do? Really! We support each other. We may have our little differences, but as soon as we know one of the others is in trouble, we help out. It is like having your own support group there all the time."

## The impact of commitment

It has been difficult to see whether the project has had an impact on the community apart from the actual furniture that many have had upholstered. We realized that people in the community seldom get the chance to hear how the co-op works and what its goals are. After a presentation of their work at a Community Lunch program, people were surprised to learn that it was our own business. They thought we were hired and working for St. Columba House. So the story needs to be told more often.

Faye spoke of the impact of their work on the many, many visitors from other communities, congregations, outreach ministries and even other countries such as Mexico, Zambia and Peru. "All these groups that come to see you, go away with a tremendous amount of energy and hope. They see, as I do, what deep commitment it takes to hang in there year after year, determined to make a go of it for both yourselves and the community. I have been aware as I have worked with you over the years, how tough it has been and how discouraging it has been financially. The work is so physically demanding and we all have been surprised at how long it takes to learn all the skills needed, but you have done it. Your work is valuable, your commitment is really an act of faith, and for those who can see this, you are a sign of hope."

# HOPE – *Shifting from Margin to Centre*

4

*Hope is a big word. It is always hope that keeps you going. So hope is the good word. In the struggles you are going to face, it is hope that keeps you going. — Myrna*

*I*n Point St. Charles we are confronted daily with the effects of poverty, the lack of education, high unemployment, isolation, domestic abuse and the deep anxiety that the future may not be any better for our children. As a group of women from "the Point," we have spent many years working with others to change the living conditions in our community and we have come together to talk about what helps us hang in as the times get harder and harder.

In a small Biblical worship/reflection group, we see this work through new eyes and seek to understand what brings hope or new energy in the struggle. The starting point of our worship is the concerns of our community, the projects we are involved in, the pressures that we are facing and the light that breaks through from time to time. We use a scripture reading to focus our questions and push us to deeper understandings of both our task and God's participation with us.

A few years ago, the "Women's Discussion Group" of St. Columba House, spent a number of weeks discussing their vision of what they would like their community to be. We spoke of our dream to have schools in our community, for both adults and children, and to have good affordable housing and enough nutritious food in each home. We spoke of a factory that would produce something of value for the community. We constructed a large collage together (that still hangs in our meeting room), working with scraps of material to build this new community as we spoke of our goals. Our discussion was like Isaiah's prophetic vision as he spoke of the emergence of a new society:

My people ... will build houses and get to live in them — they will not be used by someone else. They will plant vineyards and enjoy the wine — it will not be drunk by others. Like trees, my people will live long lives. They will fully enjoy the things that they have worked for ... and their children will not meet with disaster. — Isiaiah 65:21-23

Our Women's Group was not dreaming "in technicolour." Our vision was both simple and profound, rooted in the ordinary, everyday needs of our community. We were not content to leave this vision as a dream, but, during the following weeks, months and years we have continued to work, in spite of enormous obstacles, to change conditions in our community and to offer a ray of hope.

*What this collage lacks in beauty, it makes up for in the deep hope it represents for a better life.*

The Worship Group has moved towards a very concrete understanding of how God works to free people through sharing, advocacy, education and action for social change. Our reading of scripture repeatedly breaks open the text in new ways with the intuitive identification with the powerless in any story or encounter. It has been a gradual process for us to feel confident in the significance of our own interpretations and it has been tough to let go of deeply-rooted beliefs in an all-powerful, judgemental, male God. As Myrna has said, "It was a lot easier when I believed there were right or wrong answers and I kept hoping for the miracle that was going to make everything alright. But once your eyes are opened, there's no turning back!"

As we have named the powerful forces that continue to destroy families and community, we have found in the Bible, particularly in the actions and parables of Jesus, new understandings of God's struggle on the side of the poor throughout history. As this awareness has grown, we have wanted to find ways to reach out beyond our small group, to openly share and involve others in making their faith address the real questions that are being asked.

We began to talk of possible ways we could express through some symbol the connections between our work for social change and the gospel. We decided to make a banner for our Main Hall in St. Columba House and invited a number of the groups from our centre to participate in making it. Each group was asked to symbolize the essence of their work on brightly coloured burlap rectangles. We explained that we would sew the pieces as background around the outline of a cross embroidered on a large fabric banner.

The results exceeded all our expectations! Each rectangle is a story in itself and their creation provoked much discussion about the goals and visions of the groups. They symbolize many of the voices, the stories and the struggles we have lived through together. We will share a few of these stories that capture some of the theological insights we have had.

## The widow and the judge

When the School Board threatened to close the only English Protestant elementary school in our neighbourhood in 1985, a group of parents gathered to fight back. After unbelievable bureaucratic opposition the

Point Adult Centre for Education (PACE) was started by a group of community women to make fuller use of the school.[7] The small, volunteer committee of women, who themselves have no post-secondary education, continue to administer and fight to keep the adult centre open for the over 200 people who are taking courses.

The logo of the education centre is a woman carrying a protest placard with "PACE" on it and this has become a powerful symbol of hope for those in the community who so desperately want education that relates to their everyday needs. Their logo on the banner represents years of struggle for social change.

The day we discussed the parable of the widow and the unjust judge, Donna, who is one of the most gentle, fighting members of PACE, said, "That's us! We keep coming, pleading for our rights, until we wear them down at the school board."

> Then Jesus told his disciples a parable to teach them that they should always pray and never become discouraged. "In a certain town there was a judge who neither feared God nor respected anyone. And there was a widow in that same town who kept coming to him and pleading for her rights, saying, 'Help me against my opponent!' For a long time the judge refused to act, but at last he said to himself, 'Even though I don't fear God or respect anyone, yet because of all the trouble this widow is giving me, I will see to it that she gets her rights. If I don't, she will keep on coming and finally wear me out!'" — Luke 18:1-5

We marvelled at how this widow, who had so few rights and was the most vulnerable in biblical times, could ever have known that she *should* fight for her rights. She somehow knew that she as a woman had value, in spite of what society told her and she found the courage to stand up against injustice. This was a powerful act of faith for us and a breakthrough in understanding the meaning of this parable that could help us "to pray and not be discouraged." We knew what it was like to go before the authorities (such as the School Board or welfare bureaucrats) to fight for our rights and be repeatedly dismissed. There was no question raised in the parable about whether she was in the right, but the struggle to receive justice was a long battle. This determination and faith is the point of Jesus' message. Most Bible commentaries focus on the comparison of the unjust judge and a just God, missing the heart of this story of courage.

## The woman who was bleeding

Hours of talk and hard work went into the Women's Discussion Group symbol. We made tiny women figures out of scraps of material, much like the *arpillera* from Chile that hangs over Faye's desk. These figures are arranged around a coffee table and one woman is embracing another, who is bent over in tears. Above them are colourful strips forming a rainbow, which symbolizes our hopes and dreams. On the rainbow are symbols of many things we have discussed and shared, such as love, children, sex, cooking, money and education.

The tears, the comfort and the vision come together in one tough story. The Women's Group together had dealt with the sexually abusive actions of a local doctor.[8] The scripture passage that seemed to reflect this for us was about the woman who was bleeding:

> As Jesus went along, the people were crowding him from every side. Among them was a woman who had suffered from severe bleeding for twelve years; she had spent all she had on doctors, but no one had been able to cure her. She came up in the crowd behind Jesus and touched the edge of his cloak, and her bleeding stopped at once. Jesus ask, "Who touched me?"
>
> Everyone denied it, and Peter said, "Master, the people are all around you and crowding in on you."
>
> But Jesus said, "Someone touched me, for I knew it when power went out of me." The woman saw that she had been found out, so she came trembling and threw herself at Jesus' feet. There in front of everybody, she told him why she had touched him and how she had been healed at once. Jesus said to her, "My daughter, your faith has made you well. Go in peace." — Luke 8:43-48

When we discussed this passage in worship, we spoke of how women were made to feel unclean and how male-structured taboos isolated and condemned them. The group marvelled at the woman's courage to venture into the crowd in spite of the tradition that kept her isolated, judging her to be unclean because of her flow of blood. We spoke of the powerful faith that enabled her, a woman alone, to take action to rid herself of her affliction. We recalled that the group of women who confronted the medical director about sexual abuse did not use the same language, but their act was a similar step towards taking charge of their bodies and reaching out for healing. They too were the victims of a gender and class hierarchy that often controlled and abused them. Collectively the group of women had been able to name the fear that trapped them and how powerless they felt. They too, found the courage to take a step towards changing that and in their action there was a healing power. "Your faith has made you well."

## The workers in the vineyard

Point At Work (PAW), the reupholstery co-operative,[9] made a piece for the banner that shows miniature examples of the work they are doing now, but doesn't show the struggle it has been, the risks they have taken and how hard it is to often go without pay.

Two of the women upholsterers participated in the Worship Group's difficult discussion of the parable of the workers in the vineyard.

> "The Kingdom of heaven is like this. Once there was a man who went out early in the morning to hire some men to work in his vineyard. He agreed to pay them the regular wage, a silver coin a day, and sent them to work in his vineyard. He went out again to the marketplace at nine o'clock and saw some men standing there doing nothing, so he told them, 'You also go and work in the vine-yard, and I will pay you a fair wage.' Then at twelve o'clock and again at three o'clock he did the same thing. It was nearly five o'clock when he went to the market-place and saw some other men still standing there.' 'Why are you wasting the whole day here doing nothing?' he asked them. 'No one hired us' they answered. 'Well, then, you go and work in the vineyard,' he told them.
>
> When evening came, the owner told his foreman, 'Call the work-ers and pay them their wages, starting with those who were hired last and ending with those who were hired first.' The men who

had begun to work at five o'clock were paid a silver coin each. So when the men who were the first to be hired came to be paid, they thought they would get more; but they too were given a silver coin each. They took their money and started grumbling against the employer ... 'Listen, friend,' the owner answered one of them, 'I have not cheated you. After all, you agreed to do a day's work for one silver coin.'" — Matthew 20:1-17

The women in the PAW co-op struggle to create a different vision of how a business can be fair, while being very realistic about how hard it is to share equally when people work at different levels. We spoke of the powerful message of Jesus that people have a right to work and a fair day's wage that allows their families to live with dignity. But we know that is not how the business world functions today. It is an ongoing struggle for PAW to charge enough for their labour to be able to survive on their salaries while at the same time, wanting to provide a service that people in the community can afford on the very low incomes they have. It is a tough dilemma. It has also been a strong commitment in the cooperative that the women will share income equally, even if there is a difference in their productivity since, as in this Bible parable, they all need a fair day's wage to survive.

The line-ups in the marketplace still go on each day in Montreal, as the unemployed line up at five a.m. at Workshare offices hoping someone will come by for workers. This passage seems as relevant today as it must have been for all those people that listened to Jesus that day. Our commitment that each worker must have their basic needs met, has also been the theological basis of the salary parity policy for staff at St. Columba House and has had a powerful impact on our understanding of shared responsibility.

## The Christ in our midst

Other groups created symbols representing the many stories of struggle and hope in the years of work for social change in our community. The Welfare Rights Committee depicted their work with a "NO" sign over "Law 37," the regressive punitive Welfare Reform in Quebec. The Hot Lunch Program's happy portrayal of children eating together has been connected to Jesus' feeding of the 5000 in which the resources at hand were distributed to provide enough for all. (Mark 6:35-44)

The day came when all the pieces were gathered together and we began to arrange them around an outline of the cross. And then came an unexpected flash of insight. Melissa suggested, "Why don't we use the pieces themselves, to form the cross?" and she started to move them.

As the pieces were moved from the margin to the centre, forming the cross, we knew that it was right.

It was a very powerful moment as we realized the significance of what we had done. "Wow! That really says something!," one woman exclaimed. We had made a statement that the work of the people *is* the Christ in our midst — the ongoing presence of God in our suffering, pain, despair, joy and celebrations — the continuing struggle to build a more just community.

The creation of the banner was our naming of the Christ. It symbolizes for us that the work of the people has not only moved from the margins to the centre of the cross, but that the cross itself is at the heart of our work and reflection. This movement back and forth is the core of our understanding of the connection between the work of a community deeply committed to justice and our faith.

The banner hangs in our Main Hall in the midst of all the activities, organizing, community meals and meetings. It has become a focal point that has helped our Worship Group share with others our understanding of theology that comes out of our day-to- day experiences in the struggle for a more just society.

## The Canaanite woman

We are discovering in our community, the powerful resources to be found in the integration of women's struggles, the work for social change and the place of faith. This interrelation is most powerfully expressed through the Worship Group's discussion around the text of the Canaanite woman's confrontation with Jesus.

> Jesus left that place and went off to the territory near the cities of Tyre and Sidon. A Canaanite woman who lived in that region came to him. "Son of David!" she cried out. "Have mercy on me, sir! My daughter has a demon and is in a terrible condition."

But Jesus did not say a word to her. His disciples came to him and begged him. "Send her away! She is following us and making all this noise!"

Then Jesus replied, "I have been sent only to the lost sheep of the people of Israel."

At this the woman came and fell at his feet. "Help me, sir!" she said.

Jesus answered, "It isn't right to take the children's food and throw it to the dogs."

"That's true , sir," she answered, "but even the dogs eat the leftovers that fall from their masters' table."

So Jesus answered her, "You are a woman of great faith! What you want will be done for you." And at that very moment her daughter was healed. — Matthew 15:21-28

We did not like this passage at first. It was not just the difficulty in seeing Jesus being close-minded and lacking in compassion. We felt so connected to this woman who was an outsider, who was being ignored, whose behaviour was being criticized by the disciples as she was fighting for her child.

Donna spoke of how desperate the mother must have been to take such extreme measures. "She must have been so afraid and yet she had such courage. She had to face being laughed and shouted at, but she still hung in there. It is so like people who are misunderstood and shunned in our community."

Myrna was very troubled and said; "It feels too close to home for me. I remember how I was humiliated in front of my children at the welfare office. It is really hard to read that Jesus was putting her down too."

We marvelled that the Canaanite woman had shown such remarkable openness and courage as she had dared to look outside her own community and faith for help. She knew what was important and was willing to do anything for her child. Because she was so determined, this woman changed Jesus' mind. Jesus was turned around, converted, by this woman. We found new respect for this Jesus who could make mistakes, admit it and change.

Donna spoke of her new understanding of how much God needs us in the work of justice. "The way I see it now, it is the work and vision of ordinary people that God needs to turn people and the church around."

## Jesus' teaching starts a riot

The Worship Group has continued to look for ways to reach out further in our community and we have begun to take some chances. Last Eastertime we decided that instead of having our worship after the Community Lunch program was finished, we would hold it as the animation time, right in the middle of the gathering of over 100 people (families with small children, couples and single people, both young and old). As we announced it was the time the babies could go to the child-care room, we also explained what we would be doing and invited people to stay to participate. We had expected a quick exodus, but almost everyone remained. Donna opened with prayer and then Myrna read the following scripture:

> The whole group rose up and took Jesus before Pilate, where they began to accuse him: "We caught this man misleading our people, telling them not to pay taxes to the Emperor and claiming that he himself is the Messiah, a king."
>
> Pilate asked him, "Are you the king of the Jews?"
>
> "So you say," answered Jesus.
>
> Then Pilate said to the chief priests and the crowds. "I find no reason to condemn this man."
>
> But they insisted even more strongly. "With his teaching he is starting a riot among the people all through Judea. He began in Galilee and now has come here." — Luke 23:1-5

We looked at the complaint that Jesus "with his teaching is starting a riot among the people all through Judea... and now he has come here." Faye asked the people what this sounds like in our community and the responses came from all sides. People spoke of the G.S.T. (Goods and Services Tax) and how unfair it is to poor people. Another reminded us that we have to keep stirring people up now to fight for our rights or we would have nothing to live on. Others talked of how some of us are called troublemakers today and why people try to silence us. People were amazed that what they said was important and that others listened. It was a very moving time in which we could really understand in new ways what impact Jesus' teaching about a just society had both then and now. People talked about the Easter Service for a long time after and were very interested in how much the Bible passage related to how we live in our community and the struggles we have. So on special occasions, we have continued to make opportunities to continue this sharing with the larger community.

## Hope in the darkness

The Christmas Worship during the Community Lunch program began with the lighting of a candle as the symbol of hope in the darkness. We asked what that darkness was and people responded immediately: — "the government cutting back our welfare cheques again;" "the lack of jobs and no hope of ever getting one;" "the increasing number of people who don't have enough food;" "the social reform that is all about saving money, not about helping people to get ahead;" and "the rich are getting richer while those at the bottom have nothing."

We read the Magnificat, spoke of the dark times then and asked how these words sound to us today:

> Mary said,
> "My heart praises the Lord; my soul is glad because of God my Saviour, for he has remembered me, his lowly servant!
> From now on all people will call me happy, because of the great things the Mighty God has done for me.
> His name is holy; from one generation to another he shows mercy to those who honour him.
> He has stretched out his mighty arm and scattered the proud with all their plans.
> He has brought down mighty kings from their thrones, and lifted up the lowly.
> He has filled the hungry with good things, and sent the rich away with empty hands.

He has kept the promise he made to our ancestors, and has come to the help of his servant Israel.

He has remembered to show mercy to Abraham and to all his descendants for ever!" — Luke 1:46-55

There were comments that none of these predictions had happened yet and that we live in a tough world. So the question was asked, "then where is the hope?" There was a long, heavy silence and then from different places all over the room, the voices were heard: — "There is news that there are the first steps towards peace in Ireland." "When I see someone in the community really caring and sharing what they have with someone else, that is hope." "PACE is a place of hope for us — people are learning who never had a chance before." "People are coming here to have a hot meal together and to talk — that is like hope." "In the Middle East, Palestine and Israel are really talking — who would have thought that could happen?" As the comments came, Donna said afterwards that it was like seeing small little candles lighting up the darkness throughout the hall, until the whole place glowed!

It took ten years of meeting weekly for worship with a small group before we had built the base of understanding in the community that has allowed this more open sharing. This has given us new hope and energy for the struggle!

## Sharing our message

We have also become more involved in sharing our stories and reflections with church people outside the Point. Myrna and Donna are discovering the very special gifts that they have to convey the gospel message from a very different perspective. As we have led discussions with church groups, theological students and a Lay Preacher's course, we have had to struggle to understand how connections can be made across class barriers and have found this to be quite a challenge.

Myrna, Donna and Faye were invited to give the theme presentation at an annual meeting of the Women's Presbyterial for the Montreal region churches. We joined the women for lunch and we happened to sit at a table with a group of "old Pointers," as they described themselves. They either were born in the Point or had lived here for many years. It was fascinating to sit with them and reminisce about different landmarks, places, people and to hear what it was like before we were born.

Our presentation was on the theme "From Margin to Centre." Faye did the introduction about our worship group and how we arrived at making the banner. Myrna and Donna talked about the significance of the pieces that formed the banner, some stories they represented and how the worship group related scripture passages we had dealt with to the experiences of the community. We then told the story of how the pieces moved into the centre to form the cross on the banner and what an impact that had on us. As we unfurled the banner there was a wonderful "Aah" and the feeling that they shared in understanding what this meant. Many women came up to us afterwards to ask about the banner and it seemed to have quite a powerful impact on them. Myrna felt that "it wasn't just the banner that amazed them, but that the symbols of our work form the cross. When we show it, I sometimes feel as overwhelmed as we were when we first put it together. When we see somebody looking at it, I hope they know what we felt when we made it and that it comes alive for them."

We asked the women present to discuss together the passage of the gold coins (Luke 19:11-27) and we had a very lively exchange. We shared our struggle with this passage and how we read it as a critique of the context in Jesus' time and ours.[10] We discussed our present socio-economic context and how this passage spoke to us.

Donna recounts that "I spoke about poverty, how hard it is to live on the little the government gives on U.I.C., welfare or minimum wage jobs. The reality is an everyday struggle to make ends meet. One woman from the assembly stood up and spoke about needing to have faith in God and all will be provided for. When I tried to explain that faith is not lost because a person worries about where the next meal comes from, I felt that my faith was being questioned. I feel that because I don't pray for miracles, that doesn't meant I don't believe in a Creator who is beside me in my struggles."

Donna closed our presentation by leading the group in prayer and it was the first time that she had prayed publicly. Her words were very powerful, simply stated, gentle and strong. Many commented on her gift and this has encouraged Donna to continue in other ways to lead in worship in our own community.

And so we meet, we talk, we pray, we challenge and we dig deep to find a way to speak collectively of the sources of hope we find in our unique community. The gospel message has come alive to us with new meaning and a powerful sense of God's presence in the midst of our struggling community. As we have talked and worshipped together, we have been changed and blessed.

# 5

# HOPE *in Work: Is Work a Source or Destroyer of Hope?*

*O*ur discussion about work opened up many questions about what we call work, why we work, the effect work has had on us and the motivation to work. Elizabeth spoke of her experience working at home and the effects of different kinds of work outside the home. Her story raises many of the questions all of us have about work.

"When I had three children and Peter was nine months old, I took a job cleaning offices. My mother did it all her life and that's all she thought she could do. But when I was doing it I kept thinking, 'what am I doing here? I can do better than this. I know I can do better than cleaning other people's dirt. It's bad enough doing it at home. Why am I doing it for a living?'

"But the reason I did it was because I wanted to be home with the children during the day. I had them and I wanted to take care of them. So I went out during the night so my husband could be home with them at night while I was out cleaning. I was exhausted when I came home and I had to be up early with the kids every day. But I still felt that wasn't me. There was something better in life for me. There had to be. I didn't want to end up, like my mother did, with 35 years of cleaning offices. What got me out of it was being laid off. Three months later I was asked to become a Teacher's Aid at my children's school and I think that is what started it all for me. I was working with PACE before that, but I was still working cleaning offices then too. I think I was too exhausted to realize what PACE had meant to me at that point. I was really, really exhausted, but I knew there was more to life than that."

All of us have families and work as well, so the question of the relationship of our work to our families was very important. Donna chose to stay home with her children when they were young, even though financially they couldn't afford it. But as she looks back now, she realizes, "When I was home with Fred and the kids, I didn't know who I was. I was my parent's daughter, I was Fred's wife and our children's mother. It wasn't until I started being involved outside the home that I found there was a chance to find out who Donna is and the things she likes. Now I'm in the process of finding out who I am and to be me."

Although Elizabeth looked after her family and worked at the same time, she shared some of Donna's feelings. She liked being home with the family and even though she also was bringing in her salary, it was not enough. She says; "I didn't feel like I was contributing anything. I really was and I know I was, but at that point I didn't *feel* I was. I felt more dependent on my husband than I should have been. I didn't have a lot of confidence in myself. Now that I've been working, I'm not the same." It is clear that for Elizabeth, it is not working in itself that produced the changes in her, but the type of work and volunteer work she became involved in. Recalling a recent encounter with her mother at the Adult Education Centre, Elizabeth said; "My mom comes over and says, 'You've come a long way and I'm proud of you.' I know I am 40 years old, but I can still make my Mom proud of me!"

For Melissa, the relationship between work and family is more complex. She says, "I work because I really find it hard staying home. I enjoy being home, but I really find it hard being there. I find staying home with the kids ten times harder than here at work. I do miss staying home with the children to be honest. I feel I cheat the kids when I'm not home. I enjoy my work, but I feel guilty working."

Myrna spent fifteen years at home with her five children before she started work as a cook at St. Columba House and she says of that experience; "I found it very hard when I worked the Lunch Program here. I didn't really dislike it. It was a job. There's a difference. I'm not saying I hated it. It just wasn't rewarding. It is nice to have a job that is rewarding, or when you feel in your heart or your being, that you are doing the best you can." Even though there were rewards for us all, being home, we looked outside the home for the chance to fully utilize our abilities and feel a sense of our own worth.

There is no consensus on the relation between salary and work. Although being paid for work done was appreciated by all, Faye was the only one who found that this was very important for her own self-worth. Money is not the motivating factor in our work now. As Melissa said, "Let's face it, I don't work just for the money, because I pay half of my salary out in babysitting costs." At the same time, Melissa is most emphatic about her need to have financial independence and control of how she chooses to spend her money within the family.

It seems that there has been a shift in how work is looked at, because of changing experience. Work that was "just a job," that is, simply brought in money, was not valued. The type of work is crucial and must provide a way for one's particular skills or gifts to be utilized in order for it to be valued. When Myrna speaks of work, it is as though her paid employment is no longer classified as "work" because it is so fulfilling. It seems that underneath our discussion is the expectation that work will be tough and not enjoyable.

*Elizabeth with Glenn and Amanda in the After School Program at St. Columba House. Elizabeth says, "I enjoy my time helping children in the After School Program so much that it is hard to call it work."*

Myrna explained; "I don't know what I would do if I didn't work. My life is my work now. I really enjoy it. Work to me is — not work. To me it's everything — working with the people in "Hand in Hand," the Women's Group, the Worship Group. I love it! I guess what I'm trying to say is that my work is reversed. I feel like my work is at home now and my personal enjoyment is at work. Work is having to do the things you don't always want to do. Here (at St. Columba House) I am doing things that I never dreamed I would be able to do."

It is as though, when work becomes enjoyable, instead of a means to an end — mere survival — it is no longer seen as work.

For Donna, work is tied to salary, of necessity. She says; "We need the money to survive. If Fred was working and we didn't need money, I would probably come in and do it anyway. But right now it means a lot to me to get paid. But I could look at it in another way. If I'm being paid to make something for someone, I take the money but still get pleasure out of it. I don't think of it as something that's a job. It's something I enjoy and it is the only way I can relate to upholstery. I put my whole being, my whole self in it. I take pride in it and I feel I can give something to someone else."

Melissa reacted very strongly to Donna's words and stated emphatically that it is very hard work. Donna acknowledged how tough the work is, but that even when she is tired and beat at the end of the day, she feels good about it. Although all the members of the co-operative feel the pressure of the uphill battle they are engaged in to succeed in a business in such tough times, because of different areas of responsibility in the Upholstery Project, they may feel the weight of this differently. Melissa, as co-ordinator of that project, is more involved with the management and has deep concerns about the future of the co-operative.

Melissa said; "I look at the work differently, because it's such a struggle. The co-operative is a learning experience, but it is work because it's always a new struggle and new pressures. Sometimes I find that it is just too much. When I go home I'm exhausted, not from the upholstery, but the pressures we are under and the struggle the business has been under for so long. What is going to happen in the future is pressure, so it is like work. It is hard work and I look at it as work."

Work is seen as that which exhausts you, drains you, and takes away your energy. When "work," meaning one's employment, leaves you fulfilled and with a sense of accomplishment, then it is no longer regarded as work. The expectation is that work will sap you.

# Families influenced our outlook

Faye suggested that it would be helpful to push further on our discussion of work, looking at how we formed our ideas about work, how work was seen in our families and whether our own experiences are changing this understanding.

Elizabeth said that she believed that "a lot of it comes from our parents. Work for me at the beginning was just work and that's it. I never found enjoyment in work and I didn't expect to. That's not how I was brought up. You go out to work and do it."

Donna commented; "I remember once I visited where my father worked, but I was all dressed up and warned not to get dirty. So that's what I concentrated on. It wasn't until years later that I found out exactly what he did. He was a carpenter and built sets for commercials. He didn't talk about it. He worked a lot and he worked six days a week for long hours. I don't ever remember him complaining about his work. I remember him complaining about the long hours, but not about the work itself. If anything, when I reflect back on my father and his attitude towards work, I could honestly say that he probably enjoyed it. I think it is where I get that from. My mother worked up until she got married and then my father preferred she stay at home. She never went back to work."

Faye commented that a lot of people say you have to work to have dignity and we discussed whether our parents' work give them dignity in any way.

Elizabeth's response was very emphatic. "No, my mother's work didn't. She was a cleaning lady. She didn't like it and did it because she had seven of us to bring up after she was divorced. So for her, work was just a need. She didn't like what she was doing and she often wanted to change it. She didn't have a great education and she felt that was all she could do. She often said to us that we were going to finish high school and then if we wanted to go on, we would discuss it. We never did really go on. She wanted better for us, this is what it was. I ended up cleaning offices for nine years [at night] because I had kids and I wanted to stay home during the day. So for me, that job was work. I hated it. But for the kids, you need money.

"My mother wanted us to get into something we enjoyed and something that was more worthwhile than she felt she was doing. She never really said what, but left the choice to us. She made it seem that her work was not worthwhile, but it really was if you think of it, in some ways. My father was a taxi driver, but I don't remember much about him. All I remember about him was complaining about his work and that there was never enough money. He didn't enjoy it. He was a milkman, delivered bread and taxi driver was the longest job he stayed at. It was long hours definitely."

Myrna recalled that her Dad was never happy with his job. "I think he thought the world owed him a living. He was a brick-layer, when he worked. And the thing that is sad about that is that everybody wanted him for their jobs, because he was very good at it. But he was always so unhappy. Like everybody, he wanted enough money to live on, but he thought he worked too hard for it. He didn't work very much. He was always out of work. He had a sore back and he couldn't always work. He was a taxi driver for awhile because it was easier than laying bricks. It is a really hard job being a brick-layer. He would say, 'I built so-and-so's fireplace and do you know how many people they showed that fireplace to?' Downtown at the Paramount Theatre he would point out the nice brickwork he had done out in front. People phoned him all the time because they liked his work. But he always was looking for an easy way. Why couldn't he have done one of these jobs and been happy?"

From her home experience, Melissa said; "I remember my Mom always came home from work so tired and it was always, don't bother Mom, she's tired. Now, I try not to go home and ever say I'm tired. For my Mom, I don't think she ever meant it that way, but tired meant *too* tired. As I got older and she started talking about work, it was better. But my Mom always carried it home with her, the worries about work and carrying everything on your shoulders. As a young child, we always had to be so good, because she was so tired. We felt like sometimes we couldn't breathe, because she was tired. I was young when my father left and I don't know if he ever worked. He tells me he worked. He always talked about these great jobs — mounted police, truck driver, worked in the mines — but I never saw him work. I know he doesn't work now."

As children growing up in working class families, work was seen as a necessity to survive, but also that which seemed to sap all energy and creativity. Although there were some glimpses of the sense of pride and dignity that might come through accomplishing something through work (such as the brick-laying done by Myrna's father and the sets constructed by Donna's father that were rarely talked about), the overriding feeling was that one did not look to work to give meaning, purpose or value in life.

## Partners influence our outlook

When we looked at our own or our partners' experiences as working adults, there were very important changes in our expectations about work.

Melissa said; " Eddy (my partner) works very hard and he gets a lot of dignity from his work. As long as you work and you are bringing in the bread, that is reason to work. If I made $100,000 and he only made $10,000, it would be more important in his eyes for him to work because that is how he gets his dignity. He might not always enjoy his work, but it is a job. Lately he has been having a hard time at work. He works six days a week and he is never home. I feel like I'm a single parent to be honest with you. I wish he would let some of that dignity go. Like, you don't have to work six days a week for me to be happy with you. "

Faye asked; "But does he have a choice Melissa? It made me very angry when you told me about his trip to Toronto in the awful snowstorm, when he didn't have any choice about driving back, even though it was too dangerous."

Melissa replied; "No, he doesn't really have a choice. If he refused too many times, they wouldn't call him. During that last big snowstorm we had, he had to drive even though it was too dangerous. He drove the truck to Toronto into the storm all day and on the way back (we got the storm in Montreal by then), he had to drive back into it. Both ways he got it. It was really bad. He had to come back and he couldn't see anywhere in front of him — like, nothing. A bigger rig passed him and swished him over on the curve. It came so close to him, it ripped off his mirror. He couldn't see anything and when he finally could see he was right on the edge of the ditch. He said he was never so scared in his life, but he had no choice about driving back.

"He got home at five in the morning, after working sixteen hours that time and they called him to go back into work at eight a.m. Another guy didn't go into work because he had been drinking. The guy that phoned said he didn't have a choice. But when he got to work Eddy said, 'I do have a choice!' But he really doesn't. They apologized after to him, but he still had to work. He is finding it hard. He has to work or he won't get the jobs.

"Now he feels really used and with all his responsibilities now for the truck and the workers on the truck, he only gets another 35 cents an hour. It is really ridiculous! He only gets paid for the actual hours of work. If they don't unload right away and he has to wait around, he doesn't get paid for that. Sometimes he may be gone for fifteen hours, but he only works and gets paid for eight hours. He has a uniform, that we pay half for and it is very expensive. The pants are a blue-grey you can't buy in the regular stores and the $40 cotton shirt has the company crest on it. Now I buy the crests and sew them on other shirts. For three months we have been paying for uniforms, $50 off his pay a week. This is the last week.

"Eddy is worried when I answer the phone, because I give the dispatcher an earful. He needs work boots. When he drove in the truck through the storm, there was no heating and his feet, in steel-toed boots, froze. He had to wrap his legs up. So now he bought boots without the steel toes. He chose warmth over safety. But he is very proud and I am proud of him."

Donna's family has gone through a major shift lately and now her husband works at home. "Actually it is okay for him now. He still goes out and he doesn't have the kids there during the day. I don't think he does as good a job in the home as I did, but I don't complain or say anything. He does it and I appreciate that. When he worked, he hated it. He could never find something he liked. Fred has respect for himself and feels he is worth a certain amount and he will not work below that. Sometimes I wish he would. When he was working before, he felt good because he was the breadwinner. That was important — it was his responsibility. Now that the roles have shifted and I'm working it took awhile for him to get used to it. I'm worried that he doesn't have a trade. He is getting older and it will be harder. He used to go out every day to fill out job applications, but now he doesn't as often. He has been turned down too many times."

Elizabeth said; "I think for my husband his work is more than a job. He likes what he is doing. At one time he was out on the Roads Department tarring roads and he really hated it. He was transferred to his job now and its more than just work. When he first started with the City, when we were young, he was laid off a lot. Even when he was laid off he would be out looking for another job. He worked really hard. He never wanted me to work. He felt my place was in the home. But after awhile he realized with four children that the extra money wouldn't hurt. He is basically quiet. He talks a bit about his work, but there's not much to talk about. He talks about the people he works with, more than the actual work."

## Our community's outlook on work

We agreed that in our community most people think of work as just a job and surviving. The majority of the people just want to work and be able to provide for their family. They don't expect the work to be enjoyable. With about half of our community unemployed, the "meaning" of work is not the issue. Although we feel we have come to hope for more in work than surviving and are quite critical about how destructive work can be to both the body and the soul, we see little in government policies at all levels that can bring hope for the workforce. We are deeply concerned about cut-backs in social programs, "cheap labour" programs and low minimum wage that are making the problem even worse.

Just getting a job is such a struggle here. People really want to work. But it is a fact that when you have a family, on minimum wage you won't make as much as you get on welfare. You work all those hours and you don't even make what you could on welfare, which is 50 percent of the poverty line. But being on welfare is so degrading. There are so few options and people are very discouraged. For most people in the community the kind of work they can find doesn't make you feel better about yourself. If it did, then you might want to do it, even if you made less. But when the work is just work, and wears you out, there is very little value in it.

Women are in a particularly precarious position and Melissa pointed out that "it is a big step, going into the workforce, especially for women who have a family. At least on welfare, you know you can rely on this cheque each month. But if you go into the workforce and you have to rely on that job, what happens if something goes wrong with the job? You feel like a failure to have to go back into the system again. If you haven't worked enough to get unemployment, you feel very discouraged and degraded to have to go back onto welfare."

Donna spoke of the difficult financial situation her family is in, explaining; "I'm the only one who brings money into the house and it is not enough. We qualify for a top-up from welfare, but we feel it is a step backward. When we got off the welfare, we didn't ever want to go back on."

"I don't understand that," Melissa argued. "You work hard Donna and you need that money to survive. Even if it is only $100 extra. You work hard for the money you do have and your commitment is very high. So to feel degraded — I understand what you are saying, but you need it to survive. You need a pat on your back more than anything. I'm very proud of her for the work she does. If you need extra money from welfare, it is there for you when you need it. If I needed welfare, I would apply. If I needed help for my family to survive I would get it. I would refuse to let myself feel belittled for being on social assistance even though I felt belittled when I went to the office to apply. I would do what I have to do for my family. I know somebody else who had a welfare top-up while she worked. She had four kids and it made quite a difference to have the medical card and the other benefits. She didn't make as much working as on welfare, but she felt good about her job so she didn't feel degraded. She was making as much as she could make at that job and then she got it topped up. She felt good because she was out working."

From her own experience Myrna understood Donna's fears about welfare and its effects on her. "I've been working 22 years now and have been off welfare. But I still have that fear of not having enough food. When you think about it, it is really ridiculous, but I always buy too much food. It is an awful feeling. For many, many years I worried about going back on welfare. What would happen if I got laid off or lost my job? It is such a scary feeling."

Elizabeth said; "I would feel really belittled if we had to go on welfare. I don't know if I could, after watching my mother work so hard all those years. She probably could have gone on welfare too, but she just never did it. I don't know why. I think she gave us those boundaries.

"It is scary to watch the teens or young adults, like my daughter Nancy. She was laid off just before Christmas and she didn't have enough for unemployment. She felt really bad and she has been looking for a job, but it is hard to get a job. She has an education, but that has nothing to do with it any more. She wouldn't think of going on welfare. She finds it is degrading. I worry a lot about young people who can't find jobs now. My son Peter works at McDonalds part-time — that's not a job. He doesn't like it, but he wants money and I can't give it to him. So he has to do it."

# Will our children have work?

We all are concerned for our children and what lies ahead for them. Melissa commented; "If you really want a good job you need an education. That is not only for a job, but just to learn about the world around you. I stress that more than a job. I really missed out on learning so many things. There may not be jobs for our children to have, but I want all those options ahead of them. It is so important for the children to learn about other communities and other places where different cultures live."

Each of us has work that we feel is important and makes us feel better about ourselves. We talked about how much we wanted our children to have that experience and how much we feared there would be no place for them. If young people in our community find jobs at all, they are usually minimum wage jobs, temporary or part-time jobs with no future and no sense that the work they do is really important. With so much unemployment they have to be willing to do anything, just as Eddy does after fifteen years of work with the moving company, or they would be replaced.

We spoke of the kind of values that will be needed for people to make it in the years ahead and whether we needed to look at work with new eyes. We felt caught between knowing how destructive work so often is and yet, that without work, it is so hard to maintain your dignity and self-respect. We find it is a real challenge to be sympathetic about how tough it is to find a job and still encourage our young people to seek work with some sense of hope, while at the same time giving a clear message that they can be worthwhile if they are not working.

Elizabeth suggested; "You have to be very strong. Peter is outspoken and speaks his mind. I like that and he will probably go far. He's trying and he has an appointment with the R.C.M.P."

Donna added; "We have to tell our kids that they have to be the best that they can be, no matter what they are doing."

Faye asked; "Do we keep saying that just to work is of value, no matter what?"

Melissa replied; "The message should be that you may have to take a job you don't like and work towards another job. You have to be doing work so that you are doing something in your life. How many people in this community are doctors or lawyers? It must be very different from how families in the Town of Mount Royal (an affluent community) speak to their children about work."

Elizabeth agreed and said; " I started in a real crummy job. We have to start in something we don't like and sometimes a break comes along. Not very often, but it does. But you have to start somewhere. You can't just stay home and do nothing. It is impossible. To a point it is all right to rely on your family, but you should not be a burden. You like to see your children get out and find a job and make something of themselves. I don't think any of mine have enough push right now. But there aren't any jobs and I guess they have to start lower down to get some experience. That's the way the system is. I've geared my daughter Nancy back into school to take a couple of courses. I don't want her to feel rotten about herself. I want her to feel good about herself. She has so many interests and so much she could offer. PACE has helped her too, because she volunteers there a lot and that has been very important. She has to get out. I have seen the difference since she has stopped working. So we have to show our kids that there are other things they can do until something comes along, I guess."

## If workers counted

We began to explore the alternatives that we have seen and how we may look for different ways for people to gain independence and a sense of self-worth. We see this as a real challenge for us. The Point At Work (PAW) upholstery project has been an attempt to find a way in which people in the community could create jobs, work co-operatively, learn together and give something of value to the community. Myrna's son is working as a volunteer in the After-School program and with the teens. Through this involvement and commitment there have been some real changes in him.

Donna described how her husband Fred is starting his own small business, growing small plants in their house and planning to sell them. "That may be our future, with people creating their own jobs. But it is so scary when you see people out on the highways with big placards — 'give me a job!' or selling papers in the middle of the road." We had all seen so much of these kind of jobs during our visit in Mexico, where even little children worked night and day selling anything just to have food.

We recalled that all those years Elizabeth's mother had to work didn't make life good for herself, but there is a pride in providing for your family. We realized that for us, our work is a very important part of our life and it is very interesting, but for so many people that is not the case. Still, it is clear that Melissa's partner Eddy really finds dignity through his work and that is what keeps him going. Elizabeth said; "That's what kept my mother going. She was working, she was making her own money. She didn't get help from my father to bring us up. She hated her job. She did it because she needed the money. She was bringing us all up and there were seven of us at that point. If she didn't do that she would have had to go on social assistance or something. I think we matured better because of it."

We are deeply concerned about the mounting unemployment in our community, in Québec and across Canada. The unemployment statistics claim that ten to twelve percent are unemployed in our province, but we know that these are not real unemployment figures. People who are the long term unemployed, those who have given up applying through government employment services and all those on welfare are not counted. A couple of years ago, before the last wave of job losses, a study done by the Department of Social Affairs of the Quebec Government, indicated that *real* unemployment was 28 percent. In addition, the large numbers who are working part-time because they can't find full time jobs are counted as employed in these statistics. Lack of work is a real crisis!

Instead of programs that will look for solutions to the destructive and costly results of unemployment, it seems that new policies just destabilize the job market further. Welfare "work" programs force people to do work without paying even minimum wage and with no protection of worker's rights, while at the same time they provide free workers for businesses, school boards and organizations that would otherwise have paid for this work to be done. We feel that these so-called "training programs" offer little real training and even where they do, with no conditions to hire someone at the end of a six to twelve month welfare work program, it is more economical for a company to take on another free welfare recipient than pay for the job.

The visit from Mexican women involved in worker's rights helped us to make the connections with the broad effects of the North American Free Trade Agreement on workers. We are all trapped in a system that is set up to protect the profits of major corporations and big business at the expense of workers who are being forced to work for less (as compared to dollar value of ten years ago), with no job security.

Last year Action Watchdog, the coalition of community groups in the Point, involved us all in a study of government budgets and our taxation system. We all know we have less and less money to live on, but it was shocking to see the enormous amount of "welfare" the big corporations get in tax breaks or unpaid taxes, as compared to the percentage tax the poorest of us pay through sales tax and hidden taxes. At another Public Assembly we looked at the debt, where it comes from, why jobs are being cut and welfare programs are being used for cheap labour, and how the unemployed are being blamed for the problem. Instead of providing more help for the increasing numbers of people forced onto unemployment or welfare, we are facing serious cut-backs in social programs, health care and education. So this is leading to even more unemployment and the vicious circle continues.

## If women counted

To give us other information that might help us understand the value of work in our society, we read sections of the book *If Women Counted: A New Feminist Economics*.[11] The Women's Discussion Group had gone to hear Marilyn Waring speak a few years ago at Concordia University and it had been a challenging evening. Even though the language of economics was new and quite difficult, it had whetted our appetites to know more.

Marilyn Waring is an economist and a member of Parliament from New Zealand, who has gone to many countries around the world to see how women are affected by work and the economy. She studied Gross National Product (the measure of everything a country produces by its work) in many countries as a measure of how work is valued. She observed that most of the work of women was never accounted for. Her goal has been to get women's work counted, not necessarily by paying for housework, but simply to be recognized and valued. In every country there are resources for work done, such as in schools, social services and hospitals. Her conviction is that if countries started to count all women's work, they would be obligated to provide equivalent resources and support to do their work. This would really make a difference!

We had a very lively discussion about the sections of her book that we read.

Faye explained why she had thought it would be interesting for us to read the chapter that is an introduction to the international economic system. "Not that we need to become economists, but we do have to know how money is spent and why. If we start at the beginning by looking at the word 'economy,' it means 'how we manage our household.' (p. 18) It means your time, your energy, your money, what you need to do to produce healthy children or healthy people who can be productive."

Donna was very excited by what she had read and jumped in to say; "When we read the definition for the word economy, I was surprised, because it's exactly what we do. We're actually like economists and not realizing that is exactly what we do at home. That word has changed so much today. They don't seem to stay with the original definition of what economy means — to be frugal and knowing how to spend your money wisely. We learn that ourselves as we're going along but it doesn't seem to apply any more to what economy is today. Today it seems to be strictly an exchange of work for money and it's not necessarily about being frugal. My daughter Jessica was taking an economy class last year in high school. In one of the lessons she had to do, they gave her an example of a company that was losing so much money and the manager had to figure out how to economize. They gave them different examples such as to get the workers to work longer for less and to use lay-offs."

After a long, heavy pause, she went on to say; "For me, I found it upsetting to see it in that way. They were leaving out the workers and how much the decisions meant to them. It made me feel that the workers were being used and abused. They were not looked at as people with feelings and flesh. They were looked at as things that did a job like machines. So you try to get the most out of it you can, putting in as little as possible. The end result was to get more production, you know, without having to pay more salary."

Faye commented; "That is what they call a profit led economy, that only deals with how you make money and doesn't deal with all the other effects. That is a drastic change from the original understanding of economy."

We were encouraged to find that the book's ideas reinforced how we felt about the system and it was good to know that other people shared our ideas about work. Donna was very enthusiastic about the comment on volunteer work. "She (the author) talked about all the different kinds of work that are not recognized as productive, like informal work. Without people doing those kinds of jobs, other work would not get done. We rely on people doing those informal jobs. (p. 25) What really ticked me off was that the business of the drug addict, the dealer and the pimp is considered productive. Since his business is considered productive in economic terms, the government has to account for the money somehow. That really surprised me! It really ticks me off! He gets recognized for his part in production or whatever, yet all these people she is talking about, do not get recognized but do good work."

Faye commented; "I found the section on production and reproduction very interesting. She was speaking of reproduction as the work that reproduces people and other things of value. Reproduction for women may be giving birth, but it is not just that. It is also helping children to learn and grow. It is like reproducing the labour force and making people available to work. That is work that is not counted."

Elizabeth jumped in to say; "I like where she said 'the wealth of a nation is its children and the creators of that wealth have no economic visibility for their work.' (p. 28) That's amazing." Everyone nodded in agreement and emphasized how important that concept was for us.

Myrna interjected; "But I think that the strong point in this is the value of women. If there were no women, there would be nothing. For me that just reinforced how important we are. I don't want to say it opened my eyes — because they were open — but it really reinforced the belief that we have in women, the work they do and what they *can* do. You can't just put them in a box and close the lid. They are *out now* and going to go on. It just reinforced what we know, but I also found that reading this made me want to do more. But in lots of places it was a put-down of women, such as the comment that 'the perception of labour as a curse comes from the very old habit of [work] belonging to women and to slaves.' (p. 26) What an awful comparison! I felt like taking that page and ripping it! It's terrible! It is like a slap in the face!"

Faye agreed; "It is an important concept to think of, that the whole country functions because women do unpaid work. That is a bit like slaves. It doesn't mean you don't have any freedom, but it means that a whole system of production in a country depends on all those people not being paid. If you ever had to pay them to produce workers, like we pay teachers for their work it would cost a fortune. You don't pay mothers to do their work, to do homework with the kids at night, to make sure they are fed well, but their work is needed just the same."

Donna continued; "We were just talking about the recognized labour market and how the informal work of housewives is in the grey area. In brackets it says, 'the volunteer work is generally done by women while financial contributions to voluntary organizations — which take place in the market, are tax deductible and have special rules within the economic system — are generally made by men.' (p. 27) The men profit by giving money to support it, but the volunteer work that is depended upon is, itself, not recognized."

Myrna began to speculate; "I wonder if women's salaries are kept down not just to save money, but also to keep men's egos intact. It is not because women are not doing as good a job as the men. I wouldn't be surprised, now that I have read the statistics, that this is why the wages are never the same.

"Another thing that was interesting was the section on 'value." (p. 21) We took a lot of time talking about hope, but 'value' is almost as important as hope — maybe just as important. I can't separate it because the value of a person's work, the value of women's work, the value that goes with people caring and sharing, goes with the hope. We always talked about *hope* and the important word it was for our hopes and dreams. *Value* is too and I had never realized that. It, too, is a strong word. It is not just a little word.

"Value is a person's worth and I don't mean money. As a person, it is their esteem, their worth, their growth, their whole being. We value somebody — for themselves, for their giving, what they give for people, what they do for each other and what they can give to others."

Donna commented; "Marilyn Waring talks about knowing the value of friendship, fresh air — they mean something. They may not have a monetary value, but I was thinking of a knick-knack my kids gave me years ago. Like it may be just a little plastic thing, but it has a sentimental value. To someone else it is worthless, but to me it might be priceless."

We discussed how Marilyn Waring speaks of a shift in value, when the word is used as a money term. She explains that at first, market value was based on exchanging one person's work for another. But now we have shifted to money value that works very differently. We had a long discussion about "surplus value" and how it functions in our system now.

Elizabeth pointed out that she really liked the discussion about work, because we talked a lot about work also. "They say that work is 'an activity requiring a worker to give up his [her?] tranquillity, his [her?] freedom and his [her?] happiness." (p. 26) That really got to me. You do give up some tranquillity and possibly a bit of freedom, but it depends what kind of work you do. It is a very masculine view. But maybe my mother was giving up her freedom and happiness at times for her work. But housewives are not getting paid. It is not considered work, but they are giving up tranquillity and some freedom."

"We've always been saying when we talk about work, that we don't consider our jobs work any more," Donna replied. "It's part of our life. Whereas for many people who can't find any enjoyment in their jobs, they are giving up their freedom. Further along in the book it says that mothers who are staying home taking care of children are not working because 'no money changes hands.' The discussion about the market value and the moral value is very important. There is the market value that all of our economy is based on, but the moral value, all those other things we have talked about that we consider of value, are not tangible and don't have a price on them. This Adam Smith (the economist Marilyn Waring writes about, who has had such an impact on the structure of our economy), he is quite a... (a big laugh and facial expression that says it all). I would like to know where he is getting his information from. He says 'man [and I assume he means the male species] will not do anything out of kindness.' Only if he is getting paid will he do anything. He goes on to say he is speaking of the male gender, but doesn't acknowledge either women's or men's generosity or good deeds."

This really stirred up Elizabeth who referred to the comment that "If Adam Smith was fed daily by Mrs. Smith, he omitted to notice or to mention it." (p. 23) "I like that! Of course she wasn't paid for it. It was her job to do that. It is still a lot like that nowadays and there are a lot of men that think that way. That has to be changed."

Myrna was very enthusiastic about what she had been reading and was ready for some action. "I'd like to sit here after reading this today and think if everyone rebelled, if all the women rebelled, what would happen to the world? But I am also asking the question, 'How free am I?' I know I don't have 100 percent freedom, but is it because I block myself and don't want to go that extra step? Or am I not able to? Is society stopping it or am I doing it myself? I am going to look at that because I just felt that I have not gone far enough. This is a strange comparison, but I will make it anyway. We talk about how we do worship and now that things have changed, we can never go back. I think the same thing happened with this when I was reading this book. If I am not doing things that I want to do, why am I not doing them? Is it because I don't want to go ahead, or are there blocks stopping me? Is the system stopping me?"

We are realizing that we can't do any of this work for social change without knowing how much of it is personal change we are looking at and how much of it means we have to change our whole system or other people's values. It is very interconnected. We saw more clearly how our own ideas of work have been formed out of our experience and how strong the forces are that want to "use" people rather than value their gifts and contributions.

Our reading and discussions reinforced our belief in the value of community work — paid or unpaid — as a way to both improve the quality of life for us all and to provide opportunities for people to find meaning through working together.

# HOPE *from Global Neighbours*

**6**

*O*ur trip to Mexico two years ago has had a very important impact on our work. We participated in a two week program called Global Awareness Through Experience (GATE) that involved meeting with grassroots groups doing development work in Mexico City and out in the countryside. Five women from the Point (including the four women of this writing collective) joined five final year ministry students taking part in United Theological College's (U.T.C.) yearly global education experience and Faye had been invited to co-ordinate the group. What an exchange! We were challenged and profoundly moved by the courage and creativity of the Mexican people who seemed to be able to create miracles out of nothing. Although the poverty was so much greater, we could really feel directly what they were living, out of our own experience in the Point.

The experience has deeply affected us in our work and we will share some excerpts from reflections on the experience that were written shortly after we returned. Melissa's reflections on Mexico were of a very personal nature and she decided not to include them here.

## Elizabeth's reflections

"When I was first asked if I would be interested in going to Mexico I was filled with excitement and disbelief, but also with anticipation.

"I had mixed feelings because I wanted to go but I had my family to think about. Could they do without me for two weeks? I also had my job to consider, but there was another problem. I was terrified at the thought of travelling by plane. I had vowed a long time ago that I would never set foot on a plane. I have this terrible fear of heights and going on a plane was out of the question. I must have changed my mind a dozen times over the

Christmas holidays. My family told me to go and not to worry about them. Faye told me I didn't have anything to worry about. I knew I would regret it if I didn't go because an opportunity like this one doesn't come knocking too often. With everyone's encouragement I did go and I am very pleased that I did.

"The plane ride was overwhelming at first but then I began to settle down. Actually, it wasn't as bad as I thought it would be. It was fear of the unknown that almost kept me from spending two most memorable weeks. Sometimes I look overhead at passing planes and I can hardly believe that I was actually up that high. It may not seem important to most people but my first plane ride has helped me to realize that I can do most anything. I have overcome my fear of travelling by plane and that is something I never thought possible.

"When we arrived at the airport in Mexico, I kept wondering if I had made a mistake in coming. There were so many people and they weren't speaking my language. I no longer had the safety of my own country. Now I knew what it was like to be the foreigner. I have grown from this experience though. I find that I am more sensitive to people's needs. I now try to make a genuine effort to help them if I can.

"I felt more at ease when we arrived at the Centro Lutherano. The garden was beautiful and Marie, who welcomed us, spoke English. She made us feel at home. The fence around the buildings made me feel more at ease too. I had this misconception that we wouldn't be safe in Mexico. I had always heard that Mexico was a place that was full of beggars and thieves. I had been misled! There were beggars and thieves but there are some in Montreal too. Seeing for myself has helped me to realize that I must form my own opinions and not rely on hearsay.

"What I disliked the most was seeing the families begging in the streets. The hunger and the hurt could be seen clearly in the children's eyes. This was difficult to take. It was heartbreaking to realize that the children must grow up very quickly. Our children can grow through the normal stages of childhood whereas many Mexican children were forced to take on adult responsibilities.

"Something that touched me deeply was the two young boys who boarded the bus singing and playing their guitars. They were about six or seven years old. They were alone without parental guidance. It saddened me to see such young children doing this sort of thing, but it was an everyday occurrence in Mexico.

"The talk by Michael Picard about the Mexican economy and the international debt was very informative. I learned about the Free Trade Agreement and its effects on the people of Mexico as well as the people of Canada. I really gained a better understanding of the whole situation. When we visited the Canadian Embassy I realized that the Canadian Ambassador was trying to make us believe that the Free Trade Agreement was good for all the parties involved. He was full of baloney.

"Our trip to Ixmiquilpan was a very educational and informative one. We visited the co-operatives and saw for ourselves the work that was involved in setting up and keeping them going. The common stable was really impressive. There were seven families who took turns caring for the cows. When the cows have calves, these calves are given to other communities so they can start a common stable. The enthusiasm and the teamwork of these families are what makes the co-operatives successful. They work together to make better lives for themselves and for others.

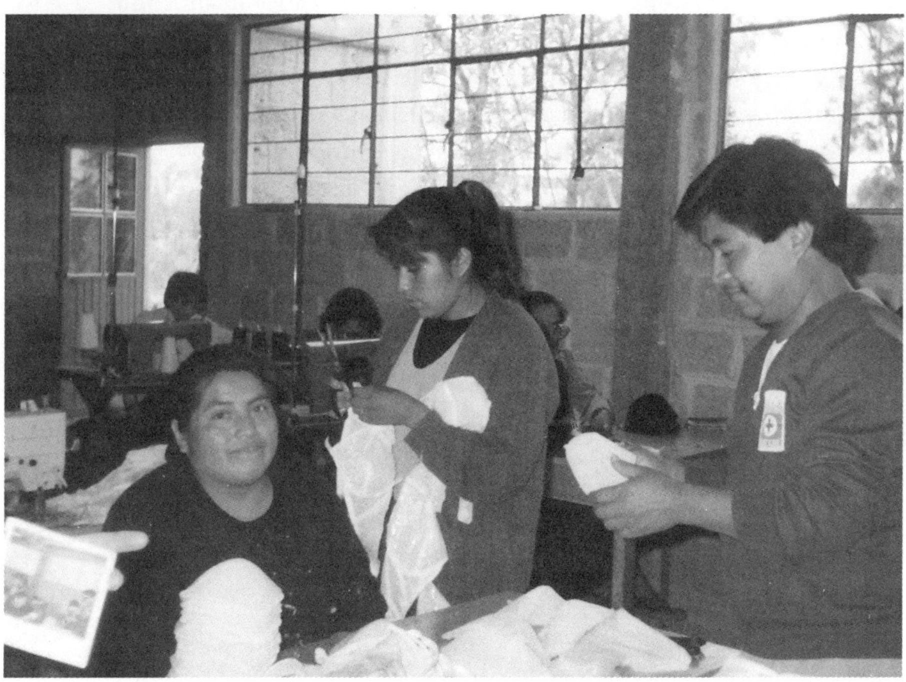

*Language was no barrier to our sharing of experiences with the sewing co-operative in Ixmiquilpan, Mexico.*

"The SEDAC Centre hit home for me. It was a lot like the people at St. Columba House. They stand behind the people of their community and help them to fight for their rights. They don't give up this fight until they get what they want or until they have at least made a difference.

"This is what I noticed at the Women's Centre that we visited in downtown Mexico City. The women there set goals for themselves and no matter what obstacles stood in their way, they overcame them. They look at these obstacles as challenges and this is why they are succeeding in whatever endeavours they undertake. Women are taking a stand in Mexico and they are getting the job done. Whether the project they undertake has to do with nutrition, health, education, culture, housing or child care, the women are making a difference and this really impressed me.

"St. Columba House is a mansion compared to their house, but we all know that looks can be deceiving. These women have drawn up a ten-year plan that will become a reality because it is the women who initiated it and it is the women who will stop at nothing until their goals are realized. This Women's Centre impressed me considerably because it hit home base for me. When we were just starting up PACE we had a lot of obstacles to overcome. I don't know how many times I wanted to give up because I thought it was a lost cause to try to beat the system. With each others' drive and encouragement, we did beat the system. We now have a thriving adult education centre in Point St. Charles and yes, it was a small group of women who started it and continue to oversee the day to day operation of it.

"I have renewed enthusiasm for our centre now that I have seen the women of Mexico succeeding in ways that were unthinkable only a few short years ago. These women didn't let anything stand in their way and it is this persistence and enthusiasm that I bring back with me. Even the women of the Christian Base Communities are standing up for their rights. Women really are making a difference.

"Something else that really affected me was the Jesus dolls. These dolls were treated and cared for with respect. When I tell anyone about these dolls and what they stand for, they don't understand. You had to be there to get the full effect of the faith. The effect was so strong that I bought one of the dolls and I tell everyone the story behind it. The faith must be contagious because I also handle the doll with respect. I feel I must treat this doll as if it were a real baby because it stands for something sacred and beautiful as all children are.

"Most of all I cherish the memory of the reflections we had as a group. I felt very much at ease during these times. We were able to say what we thought and no one laughed. The students were open-minded and very easy to get along with. They made us feel like part of their group. As Melissa said, we were very nervous that we wouldn't fit into their group but we did.

"I learned so much in such a short period of time. The faith and the enthusiasm has already affected me in my everyday life. It has helped me attempt to solve a major problem in my family and because I have grown in awareness and sensitivity from the GATE experience, I know the solution is near. The memory of the trip to Mexico will stay with me forever."

## Myrna's reflections

"In Mexico people seem to respect each other in the work they do, since they are working for their survival. Even the people who sold the gum on the metro (subway) were seen as working people. You didn't get the feeling that they were lazy and didn't want to work. At home there is no work for a lot of people. They are looked down on as people that don't want to work, are lazy and want to live off government support. People in Mexico seem to have a respect for one another.

"Everyone is so religious. I noted this the first time I went also (Myrna had accompanied the theological students on their global awareness study trip two years previously), but this time it really made me stop and take notice. As we were going through the market many people were carrying dolls. They were not everyday dolls, but special ones that were meant to be the baby Jesus. At first I just looked and then I couldn't take my mind off what I was seeing. Every time I saw someone pass by, I would watch the people's faces and how they held the doll. I really wanted to know what they were feeling. I just couldn't think about anything else.

"These dolls represent Jesus 'coming of age' when he went to the temple at twelve years old. We did a lot of talking with the women of the Point about how we all felt about it and there were different opinions. After talking, we agreed that people worship each in their own way. We talked about how much faith all these people had. I believe that their faith is so strong that the Jesus doll is looked upon as one of their children. Their hopes and dreams are part of their everyday lives.

"We were in Ixmiquilpan on February 2nd, the celebration of Jesus 'coming of age' and saw the crowds of people bringing their dolls to be blessed at the church. I will never forget this. It shows how our faith carries us through our daily lives. I believe that when times are hard in Mexico, at home or in our community, we all need hope. The Jesus doll helps people to go on and strengthen their faith, their love and the hope for a better world and life. I don't believe that it takes the place of Jesus, but is just a helping hand. Four of us brought Jesus dolls home with us.

"We had a speaker talk to us on Mexican economy and how Mexico got in so far over its head. We really thought about our own country and what is happening here. With all the lay-offs and the shortage of work, some of us are worried that the same thing might happen here.

"When we went to the countryside to Ixmiquilpan, we saw how communities worked together to get housing, decent drinking water and started co-ops for a decent place to work. They started with very few people. Some people got together from each village and decided what they needed the most. Then people put in time and labour on the week-ends or whenever they could. No one is paid for the labour and the money is put out for materials only. Communities help one another and exchange information whenever they can. The most important thing is that they gave of themselves, all they had. Sometimes in our Women's Group or other work at home, we don't want to hurt people's feelings or push too hard, so we back down. Now it is time to follow through in what we believe, even if we ruffle a few feathers.

"The Base Christian community we met with is a very exciting group of people. They apply their faith in their everyday lives and nobody is taking that from them. They know what they need to survive and they go and get it, with a lot of hard work. They don't wait for large numbers. The community needed safe gas tanks for their cooking and the gas company was not treating them right. So three women decided to do something about it, took on the gas company and won. Here at home we feel we need large numbers to take action or support a cause. Maybe if we wait too long, things will pass us by.

"Our visit in the barrios showed us how little space we need as people to live in. These people had so very little. They were happy to see us and welcomed us with smiles. They were willing to share their lives, homes and their stories. I found this part very hard, even today, as I remember when I used to be asked to tell my story of how I brought up my children on welfare. I often wonder how they felt inside and what did they think of us. Since for them, I am a person on the outside, I hope they know that I am really sincere and care.

"In every home and almost on every corner there is a picture or shrine to Our Lady of Guadelupe. It is said that she appeared to a poor peasant man, she was dark in colour and spoke the native language. She was one of them. Many people take this as a sign of Mary being with the poor and that she is there to help them through all of their hard times.

"We all went to see the Ballet Folklorico and I have a hard time to say how I felt about this. When Chucho Alvarado talked to us about the Mexican identity, he spoke of internal racism and that people with lighter skin were treated better than those with a darker skin. They get the better jobs and are seen as the right kind of people. At the ballet, we noticed that all the dancers were light skinned. On the buses and metros all the children that were dressed well or on their way from school were also light skinned. Mexican people treat their own people like we do our aboriginal people. It is time we all work together to make a change.

"The meetings with the U.T.C. students and the women of the Point were a very important part of our program. Faye helped us talk about what we saw, how we felt at the time and how we would feel when we got back home. For myself this was one of the best parts of the program.

"I feel like a stronger person today. I hope it lasts and that I can make my community a better place for all. There is a lot of work to be done for myself also. With each of us doing our best we can make a change and we can't do it alone."

## Donna's reflections

"Even with the briefings before the Mexico trip, I didn't expect to be overwhelmed with the feelings that I felt. Our first outing took us to the market and into the mainstream of Mexican life. Walking past the people who were all Mexican, of course, I felt like a minority. Our little group of white North Americans looked out of place. Then going past the men, I didn't realize how much T.V. had influenced me. They are depicted as the 'bad guys,' with their hard, stone faces. It took me a few days, but I worked this out.

"I was outraged by the cruelty of the conquest of the Spaniards. My son, who is in Grade 5, is studying about Jacques Cartier. He was telling me about his feelings of Cartier coming to America. He was not impressed and said that he thought Cartier was cruel. Upon hearing this, my husband said that Cartier was not that bad in comparison to the treatment of the Aboriginal people of Mexico.

"As Chucho spoke of the Mexican identity, I occasionally shook my head in disbelief of how Mexicans were abused and how they have learned to be prejudiced towards one another. The more European influence in the genes, the more elite one is.

"I loved interacting with the people. It was fun in the market and beautiful, also. Bartering with them was interesting. Sometimes I felt that I was taking advantage of them, understanding the hard work they put into their crafts. But then, did they take advantage of me, because I was a "tourist"? That's okay if they did.

"It is really something, how adaptive they are. They have no choice. They had to be in the past, taking Christianity and merging it with their own faith, as a means of survival. Now they have to use whatever talents they have, to live.

"The women have a long way to go in re-educating their children and men about the violence done to them. How wrong it is for them to be looked down upon. They want to have a place in the church. They are trying to take control of their lives, to have children when *they* want and trying to break the patriarchal system. More power to them!

"In Barrio Norte, my first impression was that these houses should be condemned. Then I felt guilty as I listened to how the people came, squatted there and made this place their own. The children were wonderful and followed us around. They loved the Polaroid pictures taken of them. They have a curiosity about them and have no fear. They were interested about who we were and where we came from. One boy was so thankful for the Polaroid pictures we had given them, that he presented us with a gift — a broken chain taken from his pocket. It was the only thing he had, but it was everything!

"Coming back from Ixmiquilpan, two young boys boarded our bus to make money. They were no more than eight and ten years old. I kept thinking, where was their mother? Are they alone? I have two boys that age. I kept on seeing their faces when I looked at these two boys. Even now, my heart breaks for them.

"Those stairs! How could anyone who is sick climb those stairs at the Women's Clinic in Mixcoac? Their embroidery is nothing like mine because they are learning stitches to do suturing themselves. They are really courageous. Having to take their health in their own hands is ironic because just down the hill there is a clinic that was built by the government for the community. The irony is that it lies vacant — no staff, no supplies. Just an empty building. It is there for the government to say, "Don't say I never gave you anything."

"Liberation Theology — the more I heard about it, the more I realized it is something like back home. When I first started going to the Worship Group at St. Columba House, God was distant, someone all-powerful and infinite. Me — a sinner, lucky if God took pity on me and never feeling like I'm good enough to go to heaven. With each meeting God became more reachable. The distance began to disappear. God is with me in my struggles.

"The Base Christian communities see this also. They know that God is with them in their struggles and feels their pain and their joy. They must stand firm in their fight for their communities and for their basic needs.

"Mujeres y Mujeres (a women's organization we visited in Mexico City) is another example of people taking their lives into their own hands. They have taken the initiative to better their lives. They come together from other parts of the country, in solidarity, to obtain the same goals. When hearing their ten-year plan and looking at the building they are in, one cannot help but wonder how they are going to fulfil their dream. But from visiting the groups and communities, one understands that they will. They have the strength and the power.

"Mexico has shown me the strength of the human spirit. How faith can truly move mountains. There is power not only in numbers but in only a few. Where there is a will, there is a way. Despite all the wrong done to Mexico and her people, I can't help but feel optimistic. They will not be broken. They will find the resources to use. And if they can do it, then we can do it too."

## Faye's reflections

"Over the years, we have had visits from people from many countries of the world, who have found it valuable to make connections with community organizations in the Point — the Third World within the First

World. Our groups found the visits very interesting and often kidded that soon it would be their turn to tour another country. When I gathered together the group of women who had been engaged in community organizing for years to tell them of the invitation to join the students from United Theological College in a global awareness experience in Mexico, they were stunned. Their reaction moved from disbelief, to excitement, to deep concerns about how they could ever organize their families or jobs to get free to go, fears of travel and the unknown, and practical questions about funding. It was a remarkable feat in itself to see how these problems were solved collectively. Funding was received from the United Church, the United Theological College, St. Columba House, individuals who saw the potential of such an experience and people like the cook at St. Columba House who sold baking, made on her weekends, to contribute to our expenses.

"The impact and the significance of direct contacts with people working in communities in Mexico is very evident in the previous accounts. An added dimension of this experience was the interaction between the women of the Point and the theological students. Of course, each individual in the total group added their unique insights to the experience, but there were special dynamics that came out of the life experience of the two groups. The women from the Point could identify so directly with the Mexican people we met, feeling a really strong bond and connection that transcended all language barriers. The students offered skills of analysing and articulating what we were experiencing from a theological perspective. This provided a real challenge to the whole group to continually clarify and make connections between what we were seeing, our faith and our work back home.

"The dialogue between us and the theological students was a real challenge. I think that we were able to help them "feel" the reality and they helped us to find ways to articulate what we were experiencing. There were some tough discussions and perhaps the most difficult, unresolved conflict revolved around the significance of the Jesus dolls. For the women in the group (the woman theological student included), there was an empathy with the deep significance of what they saw. Some of the students had theological reservations about the meaning of the Jesus dolls and pushed for more clarity and explanations. Two very different ways of relating clashed head-on.

"Our meeting with the FAT (Fondaciones Autonomnes de Trabajadores) was like completing a circle, since representatives from this organization had visited the women's projects in St. Columba House nine months earlier. When we walked in there was a great welcome and they showed us pictures they had taken of our work. This was the last community group we met with and they helped us pull together what we had seen of worker co-operatives, women's struggles, health concerns, workers' rights and the effect of global economic forces on all our work. We saw how they too were affected by the Free Trade Agreement, by the policies of big international corporations and governments that were directed by economic growth policies rather than the good of the people. This was certainly confirmed by our fruitless meeting with the Canadian Ambassador to Mexico who would not deal with the effects of such policies on the lives of workers and families.

"As we talked with groups in Mexico, we were constantly relating it to work we were trying to do back home, learning from them and sometimes seeing the next step that we could take. As we shared our experiences too, it helped us to see our work in a broader perspective. We were profoundly changed by the faith and the hope that we found in the work of the people. We were strengthened by the connections with other people who were struggling to improve their lives with so few resources. This experience continues to live with us as a touchstone in difficult times."

## The impact of Mexico back home

So, we came back home with our eyes opened in new ways to the struggles of our own community. On our return we shared our experiences with over 100 women in the community at our luncheon for International Women's Day. It is hard to convey the significance of this visit to others, but we know how much it is affecting our work here. We have seen how this encounter has made us so much more aware of shared struggles in other countries and we really tune into reports of world events on the T.V. or newspapers, with new interest. We discussed how the experience has profoundly affected our attitudes and work in our own community over the past two years.

Elizabeth surprised us when she said; "I never thought of this as being a poverty-stricken community before. I didn't know very much about what was happening here before. I came back and I see now that there are more people that are poor here than I thought, and they really need help. I was kind of on the outside looking in until I went to Mexico and saw everything there. When I came back my eyes were opened. I started looking at more and seeing more. Even here at St. Columba, I had seen the line-ups of people before, but it never really struck me as to why they were here (for food). Then I started realizing that there are a lot of people who can't make ends meet."

Melissa had a similar reaction and explained; "It is hard to see poverty all around. When I first got to Mexico I thought that the Point was like heaven in comparison. But it isn't. There are different types of poverty, but there are the same problems and there are a lot of similarities. There are the people that live on the streets, people who do without food, without nutrition or medical care and the violence against women. There is such a poor level of education and such high numbers of drop-outs in our community and that is linked to poverty.

"It is when I came back that I felt poor, coming from this area. I wondered, 'Have I been poor and I never even really realized that?' I never felt poor in the sense of never having any money — but then I realized that we really don't do well. We have to struggle for every cent we make and then it is gone. Now I am not working and I feel poorer than I ever have in my life. But I had never looked at myself that way before. I think that people in the Point don't look at themselves as being poor. Even though it is around you all the time — all the time — you are so used to it that it is an everyday thing. I don't mean that we don't see it, but we have adjusted to it here. But when you go somewhere else, like Mexico, and then look upon your own community, it opens your eyes more and more.

"It has been very good for me because that is what has kept me involved in trying to make changes — for myself and for other people. My work has changed since I came back from Mexico. I worked in the co-operative downstairs before, but it was just a job. I never felt the sense of what it is like to be part of a co-operative, until I came back."

Elizabeth responded very emphatically that she really understood that. "It is like PACE. I was just running an adult education centre, but I wasn't really a part of it. Now I feel more a part of it. [Everyone was amazed when she said this! Elizabeth has given years of hard work and extraordinary determination in setting up this adult education centre.] It is a commitment now. It is not a job. It is a commitment to the community. I have to be there and I have to help whoever I can. Mexico has had a lot to do with that. It has opened my eyes a lot, especially in education. I hadn't realized until I came back that there were that many people who dropped out of school here. I started to hear more and I am more sensitive to people's needs now. I was always a part of PACE, but now I feel that PACE is more a part of me."

We felt that part of the shift in our understanding had come as we talked with groups in Mexico, sharing with them what some of our work and projects were about. In speaking to others about our hopes and goals, we saw our own work more clearly.

Melissa spoke of the difficulties women experienced in Mexico and that this had the biggest impact on her when she returned home. She remarked; "I never thought of the women in the Point being controlled by men in any way, until I was in Mexico. When I got back, my eyes were opened. I never realized that women had to ask their spouses for permission to do things, for money, how it was going to be spent and the abuse they dealt with." When we reminded Melissa of the many discussions she had participated in with the Women's Discussion Group on these problems and how she had struggled with abusive control in her previous marriage, she replied; "But that was for *me*! I just didn't see that this was a problem for all the women, or at least many of them, to keep their independence or have their own minds. Physical abuse too — your eyes are closed to it. But when I saw it in another poverty-stricken community, it hit home and it hurt. Women's issues were the most important impact of the trip for me."

Faye commented that she was so impressed with how much the people in Mexico could do with so little. "The Women's Centre in downtown Mexico and the projects we saw in Ixmiquilpan really pushed me to see that we have to do more ourselves in our community here. I don't mean that we give up protesting government cut-backs and unjust systems, but I think we now have taken a different direction here as we have seen that a lot of our work must be building a community. It doesn't mean that we don't fight for rights, just wages, and so on, but it no longer has the priority that the community building has for me. Ixmiquilpan in particular was powerful, as we saw people who had milk from the cows exchange it for the cheese made in another community. When calves are born, they are passed on to another village to start their heifer project. Those who grew corn brought it to the community that had a small grinding mill, and the exchange went round and round. They have set up a sewing industry, seeking contracts from major companies, but maintaining control over their own work conditions. It has had a profound effect on me and been a real challenge to find collective ways for people to survive here."

Myrna spoke of the ongoing impact the Mexico experience has had on her and recalled; "The thing that really helped me open my eyes was the night Faye asked me to do the presentation of our community in the church in Mexico. When I came back home, it was as though I really had found my place at last. I didn't have to look any more. Do you remember how I used to say that I was never satisfied and I was always looking for something. Not that there isn't room for improvement and that I don't have to go on, but I am satisfied now. I really feel now that I know who I am and what I want to do."

Faye replied; "It is your call and it feels right now. When we needed someone to stand up in the church in Mexico to bring greetings, I looked around and everyone was turning white or looking at the ground. But when I asked you, you said yes right away. That was the first time I had seen you respond so readily and you went on to bring a powerful message of solidarity from our community. You have a special ability to communicate in ordinary words what the mission we are engaged in is about and your deep faith comes sailing through. Since you have come back, that readiness and assurance have grown in wonderful ways."

Myrna went on to say that "The second thing that was really important to me was that I found when I came home that I wasn't as shy to express myself and talk about my faith. That goes back to the Jesus doll. It made me see that people weren't shy or hesitant to show where their faith was and they used the Jesus doll to express how they felt. I still joke around, but I can talk more easily now about how I feel about God and about my work."

The opportunity to visit Mexico with a group of theological students also had a special impact. Listening to the students talk and responding to their questions about our community had really helped us. We all agreed that we each had educated each other in different ways. The students had often asked interesting questions we would not have thought to ask and so we learned from the responses of the people. Melissa found that combining learning with worship and theological discussion was a new experience for her. We all had been challenged to articulate what we thought and this had helped us to be clear about our own beliefs. We had found it easier than the students to identify very readily with the Mexican people we met, because of a common understanding between communities of struggle.

Faye commented, "What I saw happening was that the questions or the reactions of the students often pushed you to express yourselves. When there was disagreement, it was a real challenge to find the way to explain exactly why you didn't agree. You were so moved by the significance of the Jesus dolls for the people, but we all had some difficulty putting into words how we felt. The strong resistance of the students to feeling the profound spiritual importance of the Jesus dolls made you push and push to find ways to express what you felt. It was frustrating and at times explosive, but you also were raising questions for them that they would not have seen."

We spoke of what it had been like to be a minority in another country and that we had learned from this experience. It wasn't just the question of language, but realizing that we could not readily understand another culture and the ways of the people. We realized that if minorities in our community feel as much like outsiders as we did, then there is a lot that must be done to deal with this problem.

We had an unexpected surprise from the United Theological College who honoured our group with the "Prize in Contextual Theology" at their Convocation. We were proud to receive this recognition, which usually goes to a student in Theology. We had been so touched by the determination and work of the Women's Centre in Mexico City that we decided to share our gift with them.

We have been changed by our encounter with people of another country and culture. We also have found hope in their work and renewed hope in the significance of our own work.

# HOPE *Brings Change*

## 7

*We have been talking about how we started getting involved and changing. So it is important if we want to know how we get other people involved or help others to get excited about different ways to make their lives interesting, to try to understand what makes us change. Work makes us change; people make us change; experiences make us change. Fifteen years on welfare can defeat some people, but other people, like you Myrna, have moved on from there. It is really important to see what we can learn from all of this. — Faye*

*T*o have some sense of what changes we have experienced or observed and the vision that keeps us moving on, we decided to focus on our goals for change in the community. We named these goals as Work, Value/Self-worth, Empowerment of Women, Education, and Community Building. We will look at these areas to see what progress has been made, how we or others have been changed in the process, what has held us back from going further and what changes will need to happen to move ahead. In all of this we are very aware of the sense of hope that undergirds this movement and we are trying to name that hope.

Change happens both in the community and in our personal lives. Although we will discuss these aspects separately, it is so obvious that they are interwoven and our discussions go back and forth.

## Work

Work is on the minds of everyone in our group and in the community. Both at St. Columba House and in the community coalitions that we work with, work is always the number one concern. The community's goal is to provide employment that is stable with fair wages that one can live on. This goal seems more and more unattainable in the face of increasing lay-offs, plant closures and part-time or contract jobs.

The other side of the significance of work is the self-worth, independence and growth that can come from work that is fulfilling. Throughout our discussions about the meaning of work, we have focused on how much we have been changed by work of a certain kind. The 35 years of night-time cleaning that Elizabeth's mother did was so very hard on her and her family. She was exhausted and destroyed by the work itself, even if it was the means for her to independently care for the needs of her family. Melissa's partner Eddy takes great pride in his work and in providing for his family, but at the same time he is very aware that he is often abused and exploited by his company. Work that destroys and wears us out may be a necessity for survival, but it is not our goal.

## Work at St. Columba House

The Point At Work (PAW) upholstery co-operative has been a six year commitment to create employment in conditions that respect the workers, give them responsibility for what they produce and produce something of value for the community. It is fragile right now and has been a very sobering example of how difficult it is to attain all these goals. In spite of this, we have seen very significant change in the participants in the project, and for many, the way they work and the goals they are holding onto, are very important.

But how do we find hope in such a struggle? That is the tough question and a discussion we had about this, shows that there is a lot of sliding back on the way uphill. We asked if there were times we had not been able to bring hope or help people along. Faye responded that she remembered feeling a sense of hopelessness in one meeting with the women from PAW. "I felt an incredible frustration with the group. I hope you don't misunderstand this, because I think what you women do is extraordinary. It has been a long, hard struggle and I really respect that. But I felt so frustrated with our meetings for about two months. It was like you were losing a sense of where you were going. I didn't know how to keep that hope up, or whether it had been unrealistic in the first place. I felt so sad."

Melissa replied; "Well that's how I felt when I talked about hope. I'm there every day and that is how I feel all the time. That's why I said, it's a struggle. There is the hope that it will get better, but sometimes I find that hard to see."

Faye added; "We are up against many things that we can't change. But for the things we can, it is often difficult to know how we can help each other push harder at the same time as being understanding and encouraging to each other."

Myrna responded; "I was so nervous about coming back to start the year without a co-worker in Hand in Hand (due to cut-backs, the assistant in this daily program for intellectually challenged adults that Myrna co-ordinates, had to be let go). I had to push myself more than I ever thought I could. I guess what I am saying is that we really have to push ourselves — everybody. When you are down, you also have to have people to reassure you that you are okay and that you can do it. In your PAW project you have to have that. Faye reassured me many times when I didn't know what I was going to do. But I didn't want that work to close. If Hand in Hand closed it would never open again. If PAW closes, it will never open. You have to make sure that it will work. I'm not saying that it is easy — it is very hard."

Elizabeth agreed and said; "It's like PACE. You can't sit back for a minute. Registration was really low this year and I'm frustrated. I need some reassurance. We don't have as many classes as we should have. So I got on the phone to former students and I managed to get a few more. I felt so frustrated, but then you get reassured. I have people phone, like the woman that said, 'I'm 69, do you think I can take a course? I'm afraid you can't teach old dogs new tricks.' But I gave her examples of others who had succeeded and she is coming to French now. My Mom came to French when she was 70 and she loved it. It is things like that which really give me hope. You have someone coming in to read a book to you, who couldn't read before and it's so good. I tracked down two people who weren't coming because they couldn't afford it and told them we wanted them there. So they are coming to the Reading and Writing now. Some people couldn't come because they didn't have a babysitter. So I said just bring the kids. I'll watch them, I'll find a way! There's a lot of hope there. There really is. We have to work on it."

In looking at the changes that have been happening in PAW recently, we realized that the writing of this book had helped this to happen. Even though the co-operative has meetings every two weeks to discuss the work, it was describing our co-op for others that provided the opportunity to step back to look at why we became involved, our initial hopes and dreams for the project, how we have succeeded and where we have failed. This has really helped us to put it all in perspective. As Melissa said, "The discussion we had for this book was good because of what came out of it afterwards. I felt that a lot had been thought out and I felt relieved. Everybody's outlook and honesty has been a lot better since that meeting of PAW." Now that the decision has been made to make the business stable and look at the community service goal further down the road, there has been a change in how people feel. Sharing the problem with others, such as the Staff and Board of St. Columba House, has brought both understanding and support. The write-up of PAW in the Annual Report was another step and a difficult task for Donna to do. She went over all the minutes of the past years, reflecting on what had been tried, what had worked and what had not worked. She wrote, in part:

> Five years ago, PAW set out with three goals in mind:
> 1. to provide stable employment
> 2. to teach a trade
> 3. to provide a service to the community
>
> The women have worked hard in learning a trade that takes years to perfect. There is a quality of craftsmanship and pride that goes into each piece.
>
> The past year has produced growing pains for PAW as providing a service for the community has been difficult. To do such and maintain financial stability, right now, feels unobtainable. The decision to put this goal on hold was difficult for the women to make. It feels like taking a step backward. There is confidence that in the future this will be reinstated."[12]

Donna explained; "I wanted to show it like it really is, but I also wanted to end on a positive note."

Faye replied; "And you did. What I found very good about it was that you started off with the original goals. Then you said that we can't meet our goal and I think it is the first time that you have said to others — 'We can't do that.' You are always feeling guilty about it when people come in to see the project and you speak of your goals. When I saw this write-up I thought it was really good. You said clearly, we can't do it right now, but you also said that you weren't giving it up."

Myrna suggested to Faye that it seemed that PAW needed a booster to come in to check every couple of days to see that they get going. Faye replied; "I don't see that as my role. I think my role is to encourage those in the co-operative to do this for themselves."

Melissa explained; "But we have come a long way in our meetings. Before it was just Faye that ran the meetings, but it was not what she wanted. She wanted us to run them, but it took us a long time to do it ourselves. It is just recently that we were able to say 'Faye, this is what *you* decided, not what *we* decided, but we agreed with you because we weren't confident enough to disagree.' I admire us for hanging in. None of us could afford to work without salaries, but we have. I am actually more hopeful now in one way. I think that reality has sunk in and people know that either we're going to make it or not. So we will have to work that much harder."

Myrna's face lit up when she heard this determination and she said, very quietly and firmly; "The struggle is the hope. You know, it works together. You are struggling damn hard to make sure it succeeds. There is hope there. You can't say there is no hope!"

## Work outside St. Columba House

We looked at other ways we have tried to get jobs for people in the Point. We had been involved through the community coalition in approving zoning changes to allow a Club Price outlet to be built in the community. Much debate had gone on about the pros and cons of this move, but because the company promised 90 percent of the jobs for people in the region, full-time jobs and good wages, the community agreed. However, when the company arrived, the agreements were forgotten, many outside people were hired and the majority of positions are part-time. We mobilized, demonstrated and denounced in the press the turn-about and the deception the community experienced. Myrna said that "when we go on demonstrations, like at Club Price, there are people who will say, 'Look at those fools!' But I think that every bit of publicity that we do outside that people will see, rubs off on people It is not that they will understand 100 percent, but it gets people thinking."

We did not make great changes, but we did gain insight and knowledge that will help in future negotiations. This experience also reinforced our belief that the movement for change in people's lives through work is not likely to come from outside businesses.

We decided to read more on how other people regarded work and came back together to discuss the chapters "Work as Self-expression" and "Work and Social-relatedness" from Dorothee Soëlle's book To Work and To Love.[13] We felt that many of the ideas were similar to our sense of what work should be like, but that is not the reality of most of the world. We also realized that for us, when work did become something that brought dignity and meaning in one's life, we no longer looked on it as "work."

Myrna said that she "never compared work to what was said about work in the bible before, but it really made sense. I am going to read the chapters again to think about it some more."

Donna had a very different feeling after reading these sections and said; "I felt quite depressed after reading it. Technology is moving in and I think that even if people do find employment, they are going to be just more like part of the machinery. I really felt by the end of the chapter about people finding work as self-expression and enjoyment in work, that I don't think they are going to get it. That is why I felt depressed about it. That is not going to happen and I really felt pessimistic."

Myrna went on to say; "Work should be a joy in our lives and it says in the book, that 'there is no joy in our lives without joy in work.'" (p. 84) Work should be enjoyable. People should be able to do the things they really like to do. You have to get pleasure out of something. If you are in this world, you should get some enjoyment. But not everybody is lucky enough. So many people work, just to work. Now I really enjoy what I am doing and how fortunate I am. Not many people can say that."

Melissa asked; "But then who would do all the jobs that nobody wants to do? I like the plan in China that she (Soëlle) talks about, where they switched jobs. They rotated so that not one person had to do the job all the time that no one wanted to do. Farmers went into the school and learned book work and education. The teachers went out to do the farm work.

Everybody should enjoy some aspects of their work, but you can't enjoy everything about your work. I mean work is work. That is the whole point of it — it is work. To me, everything about it can't be enjoyable. I have worked in places I didn't like working, but I enjoyed the co-workers. There are other things that help you to enjoy your work such as good benefits and then you would have something to look forward to in the future or you could feel safe about the work. Even if you don't like your job, now you don't even feel secure. When I was reading this I was thinking about people losing their jobs and not feeling worthwhile. I think that it is so hard to get a job, just be happy you have one."

We talked about the writer's expectations of work, such as where she says, "I discovered the meaning of work in its three essential dimensions: self-expression, social-relatedness and reconciliation with nature by way of this experience." (p. 83) We felt that she had really left something out here. Work is also a means to survive. For us, that was the first thing. As Melissa said, "There are centuries of people who do jobs that they are not enjoying, but they are getting some fulfilment because they are bringing home the paycheque or feeding their families. People are not usually able to express themselves in their work. They are just a machine that works for their company."

Faye agreed but said; "what she is pointing out is that if work is destroying people, then it is going against what God wants for us all. It is one thing to have hard work and unpleasant work, but it may not be destroying you. I was thinking of your mother, Elizabeth. You said that her cleaning work, every night for 30 years, was destructive for her. Even though it meant she could support the family and that was so important for her, that is not enough. Dorothee Soëlle is saying that is not enough. It is like we are being sold a bill of goods now, that if you have a job you should not complain. If we start giving in to that, we are in danger. We are pushing for jobs all the time, but people should have jobs that treat them with dignity. It is more dangerous now than ever, not to hold onto some of these ideas. We are not just created to be machines that are used by somebody else."

Myrna replied; "I had a hard time with that. I was thinking of the black people and all the slaves when I was reading it. I found it really heavy. I felt really bad because they were the workers and without them America would not have survived. The rich people would not have been rich without them. It says in the book that 'If we never experience the joy of life in our work, we never mature as full persons.' (p. 84) and I felt that it was true in a lot of ways. But it could be unpaid work at home. It could be bringing up your children or whatever you consider your work is."

Elizabeth said; "I started out in the rat-race, cleaning offices just like my mother did. Then I finally decided that there is more out there than this. It is hard to change though."

We know that many people feel that there are no options. On the welfare programs, like the Extra program, people are forced to do any work and they don't get self-worth or training out of it. But it depends how those projects are done, whether you gain some self-esteem from your work. There are Community Works programs for people who have to pay off a fine or a penalty for something they have done. Some people have benefitted from the experience and really have felt good about themselves afterwards. Myrna spoke about a youth who worked off his hours with the Day Camp. "We had a letter later on from his parents to say that was the best thing that had ever happened to him. He moved on to finish his education and he did something wonderful afterwards. He was included in the whole Day Camp team and that really made a difference. That is where community comes in and I really liked the section of the book that talked about people and community. You can't do one without the other. I really enjoyed that. I think that this was a great article. I enjoyed especially when she talked about work as community. I thought that was great."

Melissa jumped in with a practical reminder; "I think she somehow missed the work that goes into that community. It doesn't just happen. I think if by some miracle we got a big plant here in the Point, it started up and everybody got good jobs, I don't think people would ever forget the need for community. I think that because we have been down and out, and know how well the groups work together we wouldn't let it go."

## Value and self-worth

In our discussions we have come back again and again to the value of much work that is done that is not paid employment. Rolly's years of work in welfare advocacy, after a heart condition that made him unable to work forced him on welfare, is a marvellous example of changing understandings of work.[14] The Women Against Contamination (WAC) committee are finding a sense of purpose and worth through their research and involvement in this work to ensure a healthy environment.

The Women's Discussion Group spoke of the very significant changes in people's lives through volunteer work in responsible positions in the community. The group itself has also been a real vehicle for change through long term support and encouragement. One woman laughed as she recalled a very special victory; "Do you remember Joan talking about not being able to cook? She really couldn't cook anything. She just opened tins for every meal. She cooked absolutely nothing, even though she had two children. It was a standing joke and everyone laughed about it. But then after awhile, the group started to take her on and help her deal with it. They brought in easy cookbooks. They phoned her to tell her step by step how to do things. I'll never forget her coming in saying, "I did it!" the first time she made a cake. She really learned how to cook and then invited the whole group to her home for a turkey dinner. The difference came when people really took her seriously. It was like a block and I don't think she would ever have got through it without the group. And she went on from there to deal with a lot of other problems." The change that we saw in Joan was really a source of hope for others in the group. They lived through someone breaking through a barrier in herself and also discovered the power that they had themselves to really make a difference in someone else's life.

Elizabeth spoke of how work had changed her and brought her new confidence in herself, but that it was not tied to salary. "Now that I've been working, I'm not the same. At Westmount Park School they call me a Teacher's Aid, but that's a phoney title. I'm not there for the teacher, I'm there for the kids. I am braver, and that's because of you. So I've told the teacher I'm not there just for her. Ten years ago I would not have done that. I have more confidence in myself than I have ever had and I have really changed.

"Even when I was working for PACE and wasn't getting paid, I felt good about myself. You asked me why I have spent so much energy in PACE over the years. I've never thought about why. I just see there is a need and I like to be able to contribute something for others. PACE is important in the community now definitely. I guess it is the rewards too — you see somebody from the Reading and Writing class who can read now and it makes me feel good to be there and be a part of it. In the beginning PACE was a commitment but if I left, somebody would take my place. But now it is a part of me and has brought my life real meaning. The hope is always there and God is the hope.

"This is where it is changing now, for my family. My children have grown up with PACE. They help out by making posters, pass out brochures door-to-door and in many other ways. It is amazing how they are involved! They go to Westmount Park School and they see what I do there as a Teacher's Aid and very often they ask how the kids were at school today. I think this is where we are changing things, with the next generation."

Melissa speaks of being a part of St. Columba House for as long as she can remember. Being involved in community activities and the struggles to make it a better place, are a part of her life that must also be having its impact on her children. We realized that when we spoke of unpaid work and activities that give one a sense of self-worth, that the connection to its value for the community makes all the difference. Otherwise it remains a way for an individual to develop, which is good, but is not rooted in the bigger picture. This larger struggle is the root of the hope that people find as they are engaged in the work for social change.

## The Empowerment of Women

> *If all the women rebelled, what would happen to the world?*
> *I'd like to tell people to do that. I wish we could just say —*
> *Okay women, that's it! Our work has to count, so just don't do*
> *all that stuff and see what would happen. — Myrna*

In our community, it is mostly women who are involved in the organizations and groups that are working to change living conditions. We realize that, on the one hand, this makes our work easier because we really enjoy working with other women and, on the other hand, the more we change and move forward on our own, the more difficult it will be to engage men and women together in the hard struggles ahead. But for now, we have focused on the particularly vulnerable position of women in an impoverished community and how we have felt empowered to take more and more responsibility for our families and our community.

It is definitely through involvement in hopes and goals beyond ourselves, that we have come back full circle to the question of who we are, as women. We accept our roles as wife, daughter, mother, and all too frequently, find out much later that we have lost sight of who we are and wish to be. When we became involved in other goals, it challenged everyone else's expectations of us. We discussed how these changes in ourselves have been affecting our relationships within our families.

Myrna spoke of how she feels put down by her family back home in New Brunswick — parents, brothers and sisters — who don't seem to understand the changes in her and don't understand her work with the Women's Group. Her daughter Melissa jumped in quickly to point out that "It is *WOMEN'S THINGS* (said with great emphasis!), that they don't understand. It is not that they don't understand, but they envy you for it and the women don't want to say too much because they might be heard. They don't deal with it. It is easier to ignore it than to get into an argument."

## Women's Discussion Group

We discussed our impressions of the write-up for this book that was done with the Women's Discussion Group and some of the changes we had seen over the years. Donna spoke of a very important change that she had seen in how Myrna and Faye function as co-animators of the group. "For the past few years I have seen you (Myrna) taking over at times and I have sat back and thought, 'Wow, she is great to take initiative and to be leading and animating the group.'" Myrna appreciated the comment but said she still was uncomfortable about doing it. So the group reminded her of what a marvellous job she had done organizing the memorial service with the women on her own when Faye was away. Myrna insisted that she had needed Faye's help to pull it together at the end, but it was clear that it was all set and all that she needed was just a little encouragement that it was going to work.

With great delight Donna recounted; "I had fun just standing there watching Myrna tell Faye what was planned and Faye just wrote it down. What a role reversal!" We all agreed that this was what our work in the group was all about and this was a great success.

Melissa said, "I found that I used to think that we accomplished a lot as a group, until we went to Mexico. I learned to appreciate the women's groups in Mexico and how much they worked together. When I came home I found myself saying — well that's my goal now, to work as a group for issues as much as they do. We are active here, but they have to struggle just for the basic rights. It was totally different. I wanted to learn more and more about them. It was so interesting. I didn't want to compare it, because it is a different situation altogether and it was a different environment. But I was envious of the women's group in Mexico.

"That is one reason I have become so involved in WAC (Women Against Contamination). It is very important work. When I started, I never realized how big a job it was going to be and how much learning and research we would be involved in. I still feel that I am never going to know enough about it, but we are learning together."

Donna commented; "A few years ago we went on a women's retreat and we talked about women's goals, the Bible and society. In the workshop discussion I realized that I had always taken it for granted that everybody had groups such as ours to go to. But after talking to one woman in the workshop about our Women's Discussion Group and St. Columba House, she said 'Wow! We don't have anything like that.' Because of her saying that I came to appreciate and realize that it is not that common. I felt sorry for her that she didn't have such support or resources to fall back on. The conversation I had with her has always meant so much to me. Our group is very important."

Myrna added; "I think our Women's Group helps make our community a better community. I'm not saying it is perfect. If there is an issue that comes up, such as housing, or having to do with the streets, or rents, or our library, we really get involved. We work to make our community a better place to live."

Elizabeth responded; "When I read this about the Women's Group, it seemed a lot more important than I thought it was. I knew about the group, but you seem to be doing more than I thought. I didn't know that you actually went out in the community and did things. The only thing I knew about was going to the doctor,[15] because I remember hearing about that. I really thought it was just discussion. I am getting the impression that for a lot of the women they started out to just get out of the house and socialize, but it became more afterwards."

Faye replied; "All these years, we have pushed to get people to ask the first questions. It isn't necessarily to get involved in something, especially at the beginning. For instance, last week we had a very good discussion that dealt with some very strong issues. We had an outline of a woman and each person had big circles on which they wrote what it meant to be a woman. We then attached them on the woman and talked about what it meant. It was a wonderful discussion and we built up the picture together — love, creativity, tenderness, confidence, menstruation, children, sexuality, strength. Each woman discussed what the words meant for her. Somehow actually saying things, makes a difference."

Some members of the Women's Discussion Group were called names because they came to women's meetings and did things that were important for them. Women have been called lesbians and accused of getting together for other reasons. In our community this seems to be the way for men to put women down and not deal with problems that exist between men and women. They are afraid that they will lose their positions and their power. It is hard to take and sometimes people just back down.

Faye commented that "Whenever we push for change we know there is going to be a reaction and fear and resistance. Any change forces other people to change. If we want to take more space, somebody has to give up space. Every time we try for change in the community, we know there is going to be resistance. So we had better understand who it will be and why. We hope we won't be producing changes where a lot of people are going to lose, but they may feel that they are going to lose."

Women are afraid to rock the boat and often live in fear. Some women spoke of being beaten when they pushed for their husbands to participate in domestic labour. For a lot of women who start pushing for that sharing, it is dangerous. But women are getting stronger.

### "Two hands for the clock"

We had all read a chapter by Meg Luxton called "Two Hands for the Clock: Changing Patterns in the Gendered Division of Labour in the Home,"[16] in a book called *Through the Kitchen Window: The Politics of Home and Family*, and found that it really helped us identify what some of our problems in making these changes were. Some of our discussion brought out how we had changed, what obstacles we had met and that for some of us there is still a long way to go.

Elizabeth jumped in to say; "I'm the *one* hand for the clock. I don't have a second hand on it right now. I do not get help at home, whatsoever.

So after reading this — boy! — I couldn't believe it. I work outside the home too, so I should really get help at home too. But I always used to say 'Well, my husband works too, so why should he do any dishes or anything? The kids were in school all day, so why should they really?' But reading this really made me think. You know, we're going to have to have some changes! (Great laughter, thumbs up signs and encouragement from all! — "All right Liz!") Seriously though, I rush home between school and PACE to make supper. Why can't one of them start supper? I don't think my husband has ever touched dishes in his life because that is the way his mother brought him up. So that is part of the problem, I'm sure. There are going to be some changes!"

We mentioned that there had been many discussions Elizabeth had been involved in about working for more equal sharing in the home and we wondered what had made the difference all of a sudden. She felt that reading about someone else with the same problem had really made a difference.

Myrna added; "Maybe you were ready to hear that now too. If you just read it cold, I don't think it would have done anything."

Elizabeth replied; "Maybe not. I am a little more vocal now and that makes a difference too." So often we have observed that taking on responsibility in one area of our life, began to push changes in many other ways.

Donna spoke of how reading the article was like a flashback for her, to how life used to be. "The writer was talking about what women felt their place was in the home. These were women whose husbands are head of the household and the breadwinners, et cetera. That was me a few years ago. I honestly felt like they did about women going out into the workforce, getting their own jobs and speaking out. They were rocking the boat and that was why people were getting divorced. I really honestly felt that way and it made me rethink why. I grew up in a situation in which I did the dishes and my brothers didn't. There were two different sets of rules for boys and girls. I was encouraged to go ahead, but that difference was always there. It also goes back to the church and what was expected of us there. I really feel that the church depicted women as if they were to be subordinate to their husbands. It kept women in their place and this is all part of the patriarchal system.

"Now that I am working, Fred is Mr. Mom, except for the laundry. Reading this article started me thinking about the laundry. I always say I do the laundry because I like it, but I think it is really like some of you not wanting to share the kitchen. It is just a little bit of power. What if I just gave that to Fred? If Fred started doing the laundry I would have no housework left. I would feel very detached from the house. I wouldn't be needed. I made a little embroidery that said 'this is Donna's kitchen.' Fred insisted that I make a new one that says 'this is Fred's kitchen.' I told him I would compromise and put up 'Fred and Donna's kitchen.'" Change has its cost.

Elizabeth pointed out that we are making important changes with our children's image of what women do. "When you are working and involved in other important activities in the community the children look up to you more, I think. They think of you as being more than just a mother. My kids have often said, 'Mom, you're a Supermom. How do you do it?' I just do it because I want to and I don't have an answer for them. It is hard to explain, but they notice what you are doing and I think it makes a difference."

Melissa found the article very negative and did not like the portrayal of women as manipulative and tiptoeing around. There was little discussion about ways women have changed relationships and share work with their partners. Although the chapter was interesting, challenging and helpful in our discussion, we all felt that it seemed to be the result of a survey of middle-class women. Women who are on their own and those who live in poverty would not have answered in the same way.

Melissa insisted; "I think the women of the Point would come out a lot more independent and stronger. This book was from people who had money and husbands. The community here is different. It is survival. People are more independent and do what they do because they have to. If they stay home to look after their children, they collect welfare because they have no choice. Society is not offering any other choice for them."

## Hope for women

We came back to the goals that we have for women in our community, what has brought some change and what the next steps might be. We share, with women of other economic levels, the goal that women must have equal pay with men for equal work and that women's jobs should be paid as much as men's jobs of the same value. Of course we know that is the big catch — that word "value." But it is hard to get worked up about this as a goal when no one can get jobs of any type.

Women need work that they are going to benefit from, enjoy and be happy in, to get a sense of self-worth. So many women have given up trying to get jobs and those in the community who are working, are very often in assembly-line work. Very few women will find the way to develop self-confidence and independence through paid employment. We feel that we have been very fortunate in being paid to do work that we enjoy, that brings us a sense of power and responsibility over our lives, in settings that allow us a great deal of independence. However, it seems to us that there is limited chance that this will be possible for very many women in our community.

It is the work that women are actually doing now, that must be valued differently. For women who are at home raising their children, whether by choice or necessity, we must find ways to give them the help and support they need to feel good about what they are doing. In groups such as the Women's Discussion Group, the School Committee and the Alternate School Parents Group, there is such openness to learn from each other. But sometimes it is such a struggle, there is so much pressure and it feels like there is no way out. The daily toll of living in poverty is so destructive and we searched for solutions that might decrease the terrible burden on so many families.

We talked about the real rebellion of women in Quebec in the sixties who stopped having the ten or twelve children that had always been expected. Now Quebec has the lowest birth rate in Canada and the government is very concerned about this. A society needs children and the women in our community certainly want them. For many, children are their whole life. We asked the hard question of who should provide for these children and for the parents that are needed to care for them?

Since so many of the families are cared for by single parent women, there was a suggestion that fathers should be held responsible. A deluge of reasons — the fear of abuse from former partners, the lack of resources of many of the fathers of the children, and the unwillingness of many women, for the sake of money, to be back under the control of men they could not live with — made this a very unwelcome solution.

Many women do stay in relationships that are abusive and they have no hope of changing. We looked at what holds us back from making changes and taking charge, and felt that most often it is fear. It is fear of change and fear of what might be lost. There is also a great fear of being alone and we recognized that a number of us had faced this. "It was fear that kept me in my other relationship. I was really nervous to actually make the step to leave. That's why you wait so long and put up with so much. It was so bad before, but once I left it was so easy. I didn't have any money, but not having to have a man come home and run me down, was like heaven to me. Decisions I made, even if they weren't the best, were made by me."

For the sake of their children and themselves, a lot of women choose *not* to have fathers involved and would rather live in poverty than continue a destructive relationship. We see this as a very important option that must be supported, but it remains unacceptable that so many women and children are punished so severely financially for this decision.

There were strong feelings that society, through government social programs should take responsibility for children. Compared to the many senseless things money is spent on, it is felt that we can afford to pay for children, if we get our priorities straight. After a lot of debate the following suggestion was made. Women should get paid a salary for raising children. A mother who chooses to go out to work, should receive an allowance for child costs as well. Whoever stays home to do this work — the mother, father, grandmother, friend, sitter — should be paid. Family allowance is for the needs of the children, but the woman or other caregiver needs money to survive on as well.

It comes back to the discussion of Marilyn Waring's analysis that we must work on what we value in society and then find ways to supply the resources to support these values.[17] Our part, we decided, is to help our community really value the work that is being done now by women (caring for children, for other family members, volunteering in community programs) and to encourage women themselves to recognize how important their "work" is. We have seen this awareness growing, but without the means to do this work well, women will just continue to be blamed for reproducing failure and poverty.

## Education

This is a major goal for our work in the community. We saw how each of us had been changed through education in a larger sense. The involvement in the Alternate School at St. Columba House had been a first step in our interest in the work of social change in our community. This school for three and four year old children is "alternate" in the sense that it requires the direct involvement of the parents in the school. Parents take their turns to work with the teacher in the classroom and there are weekly meetings of all parents to discuss community issues, health and education. Parents and children have activities to promote learning together. So the education is focused not only on the child, but the whole family's involvement. In our community, where so many parents have not been able to go far in school, this can be a very important step in encouraging further involvement in education.

Melissa shared how important this has been for her and said, "I consider myself to be so lucky to have been able to participate in my children's pre-school years at the Alternate School. It has helped me learn how to spend good quality time with them. This year's new parent-child activity program has made such an impact on me and my daughter who is in the school now. Playing a real role in my children's education is something my children and I will never forget."

But it is more than formal education that is our goal. As Myrna said, "Education should be work on the gaps. It must be linked with work and respond to what people need to know." The goal for PACE was to use more challenging popular education methods from the beginning. But it is only now that we are starting to look at that. At the beginning nobody had the time. It was a fight to keep alive, to pressure the school board and the City to establish the centre with some stability. Now, the time has come to start getting into the kind of education PACE has wanted to do from the beginning. It took that eight years to get to that point. It doesn't mean that the education hasn't been good all along. It has been wonderful and has had a powerful impact on so many people's lives. But we have not been able to do all we had hoped for, in terms of being more involved in making changes in the community. Maybe things need to be relatively stable before you can move on to that.

Donna explained that this is the goal that PACE has been working towards and why they are moving into popular education methods now in many of the classes. She said that "Popular Education is empowerment for change." You can't *give* people empowerment but it can come through their engagement in activities or groups that understand this as their goal.

Myrna agreed and went on to say; "It is giving people a chance to change. It is awareness. It kind of all goes together. But it is not forced on people or sneaked in, but happens in everyday involvement. Like at PACE, it is not something forced on them, but education that relates to their own lives. It is work on people's self-worth for themselves. People are the important part of our life and community."

Education in all its forms has been so vital for us all in helping us to both change personally and to follow our goals for the community. We need to continue to develop participatory learning in both direct education (PACE and Alternate School) and the more informal learning that goes on in many of the programs that are aimed at developing a knowledgeable community base.

## Community building

The weekly Community Lunch program at St. Columba House is a place where the activities, struggles and goals of the Point are discussed. There are education sessions on welfare rights, the social reform policy, housing problems, legal rights, women's concerns and the needs of youth. These are often animated by community groups and the goal is to develop a broader awareness of all that is going on in the community and the outside forces that affect us.

*The Community Lunch program, like the cross, is at the centre of our work.*

This program has only been going for two years now and we discussed the effect it has already had on building community. Melissa is very enthusiastic about the impact of the daily Family Lunch program and commented "We are getting so many people now. When it first started, a lot of people thought it was just a meal for families on social assistance and they were embarrassed to come. Even though they may be on welfare themselves, they don't want to be labelled. Now that it is known that everyone is welcome to come, it really helps. People are coming because they can afford it and it is a full hot meal.

"Besides the food, it has become a place where people of all ages come to meet each other, to find support and just be together. I find that a lot of people who don't usually have that chance, get the opportunity to mix with other people. They might not be the type to go to a demonstration, but now they are becoming more at ease about being involved, through the Community Lunch program. We have also brought up issues that would not normally be brought up in other large centres, like drugs, racism, violence against women, International Women's Day. I find it is like having a live, weekly Newsletter through this program."

We have seen a steady growth in active participation in the animation time over the past two years and people who never expressed themselves before publicly are now willing to take the microphone and enter into the discussion. There are new people coming who have never been involved in community groups and they, in turn, are bringing others. People involved in community projects have a place to discuss their goals, their hopes and their struggles. This sharing is both producing change in those who are learning to speak of their work and building up hope within the community as we speak of these visions together.

There have also been significant changes in relationships between francophones and anglophones who come in contact through this lunch program. Animation is usually done in English, but there are people sitting nearby ready to translate when needed. Sometimes presentations are in both languages and since we invite different groups to use this gathering as a place to mobilize or educate, we have more input now from groups that function only in French. This has increased their awareness of the significant anglophone population and together we are building a stronger base.

As we talked, we recounted the changes that we see in the larger community. With socio-economic conditions worsening and every indication that this trend will continue, there has been an intentional strategic shift that has put the focus on encouraging collective involvement and finding ways to build community. Action Watchdog, the coalition of community groups, in addition to organizing sessions on the Social Reform (which over 300 people attended) and electoral candidate debates, has planned wonderful community celebrations such as "Festi-Pointe," Hot Dogs in the Park, Corn Roast.

On a larger scale, the "Bread and Roses — Women's March Against Poverty" that began May 26 and ended ten days later in Quebec City on June 4, 1995, has brought us all new energy and hope. Women of all ages, races, cultural backgrounds, languages and social classes joined together in a common cause. As we arrived at the Olympic Park at the end of the first morning of the march, we were greeted with tables of home-baked bread with beautiful roses interspersed. As thousands of people rested on the grass sharing the warm bread and lunches, someone commented that it was like the biblical story of the feeding of the five thousand. We were truly blessed!

*The Bread and Roses Women's March Against Poverty — a celebration of women's strength and determination to eliminate poverty.*

For all who participated in any way in the ten-day march — through discussing the objectives in community groups for months ahead, walking together along the highway, welcoming women in their homes along the way or joining with the 20,000 people on that final wonderful afternoon when the 800 women marchers arrived in Quebec — this will remain as a milestone in our fight against poverty. The songs of solidarity came alive!

As we shared many other ways the community has found to pull together and looked for the resources amongst themselves to make life better, Myrna commented; "When we go back and think of where the community came from, how it has struggled and where it is today, it is very impressive. It is the struggle of the people to survive. That is the hope!"

## HOPE as the seed for transformation

In the present socio-economic crisis in our country, we see no signs of hope that there is a will or determination to work for a more just society. Even as we see the importance of people finding self-worth in non-paid work, we know that this is not the way it should or could be. We are very fearful that the continuing cut-backs in social programs and support for people who do not have paid employment will push people to spend more and more energy on mere survival. This is an enormous challenge to impoverished communities like ours. Community building is essential if we are to survive this onslaught and continue to be a community with spirit and hope.

Involvement in the community is like the groundwork for change. Through the day-to-day work together, we have seen that people begin to believe that their work is needed and that they can make a difference. This can only happen where hope already exists for a better future, and in acting on this conviction hope is seen.

How one maintains this hope in the midst of a society engaged in dismantling the social networks we have had, has been an ongoing concern for the Worship Group. We have wrestled with a passage that seems to us to lift up this hard reality and challenges us to find a kernel of hope in a very bleak context. Jesus told his disciples the Parable of the Gold Coins at the end of his ministry and it raises many questions for us.

Jesus continued and told them a parable. He was now almost at Jerusalem, and they supposed that the Kingdom of God was just about to appear. So he said, "There was once a man of high rank who was going to a country far away to be made king, after which he planned to come back home. Before he left, he called his ten servants and gave them each a gold coin and told them, 'see what you can earn with this while I am gone.' Now his countrymen hated him, and so they sent messengers after him to say, 'We don't want this man to be our king.'

"The man was made king and came back. At once he ordered his servants to appear before him, in order to find out how much they had earned. The first one came and said, 'Sir, I have earned ten gold coins with the one you gave me.' 'Well done,' he said; 'you are a good servant! Since you were faithful in small matters, I will put you in charge of ten cities.' ... Another servant came and said, 'Sir, here is your gold coin; I kept it hidden in a handkerchief. I was afraid of you, because you are a hard man. You take what is not yours and reap what you did not plant.' He said to him, 'you bad servant! I will use your own words to condemn you! You know that I am a hard man, taking what is not mine and reaping what I have not planted. Well, then, why didn't you put my money in the bank? Then I would have received it back with interest when I returned.' Then he said to those who were standing there, 'Take the gold coin away from him and give it to the servant who has ten coins.' But they said to him, 'Sir, he already has ten coins!' 'I tell you,' he replied, 'that to every person who has something, even more will be given; but the person who has nothing, even the little that he has will be taken away from him. Now, as for those enemies of mine who did not want me to be their king, bring them here and kill them in my presence!'" — Luke 19:11-27

When we first discussed this passage, Donna responded very emphatically; "There is no hope! Jesus' parables always have a happy ending, but this one does not. It started off saying that the people thought Jesus was going to tell them what heaven was like, but he told them this. This is the opposite of what he usually does, which is to teach something, give hope, present a moral to a story. But this doesn't have that. It sounds just like what is happening today. The people didn't want this man to be king, but he became king anyway. It is like our governments that we didn't want in the first place. Then the king condemns all those who were against him."

Myrna was disturbed by the passage and commented; "It is also very frightening and threatening. It seems like today. The rich get rich and the poor get poorer. That is what it says at the end of the passage. When you have money, you just want to make more. It is a vicious circle. It is like with education. If you have a good education, you can get a good job. If you have poor education, you get a poor job and you can't go on to get education."

Faye added; "I was struck with how straightforward that servant was who said that he was afraid of the king because he was a hard man. It is like people here who say things straight out about what it is like in our country."

Melissa interjected; "I see it, not as government, but as someone who is crooked who controls others. The servant that lost the money at the end didn't want to be involved in the action whatsoever, because it was crooked. It is like the poor people who stand up for what they believe."

This brought the discussion into our own community and Myrna commented; "It took tremendous courage for the one man to stand up and say that he was scared of him. It sounds like the welfare people and the 'Boubou Macoutes' (the welfare investigators in Quebec who have the legal right to pry into people's private lives and to demand information from such people as neighbours, priests, bankers and corner store owners about welfare recipients). They have the power to say whether you will get a cheque or if you are going to get cut off welfare. People can't always be as honest as they would like to be. Our system is set up to keep people down. When I went to Mexico and Bolivia, I realized that their governments wanted to keep the people down. I hadn't realized it as clearly before, but now I see how much our government wants to keep us down too."

We came back to this passage many, many times, because it bothered us so much. We began to understand it differently. Donna pointed out the importance of the passages that came before and after this parable. Jesus had just encountered Zaccheus, the rich tax collector, who decided to give half his belongings to the poor and pay back all those he had cheated. The passage right after is Jesus' triumphant entry into Jerusalem. The people were looking for a miracle or a magic solution.

Donna suggested; "I think Jesus was trying to say this is the real world. This is it! This parable is about how it is and you are living it now. The people believed the Kingdom of God is about to appear and everything is going to be Wow! Everything is going to be cool now! Jesus is here and we are going to have a new world. But in this parable he is saying that this is life. This is how it is. The rich are going to get richer and the poor are getting poorer. People are going to get into power that shouldn't be in power because they don't respect others and are only out for themselves."

Faye added, "The enemies of the king were killed. When Jesus went to Jerusalem, he was like an enemy to the king. It seems that the king is used symbolically to speak of the leaders. Jesus stood up to the unjust leaders in the state and in his religious community, and he was killed for it."

Myrna responded, "It is like Martin Luther King and others who have stood up for the rights of the people and are killed for it."

Faye said, "Zaccheus had a personal conversion and gave half his money to the poor. That was great for Zaccheus and he said if he cheated anyone he would pay them back. But that didn't change why people were poor. The system remained the same. We don't know how Zaccheus got rich."

Myrna quickly added, "But he still had enough left for himself. Some people give donations to help out, but if it doesn't change the basic problem, it won't change very much."

Faye went on to say, "In the parable, the man who spoke out against the king said, 'you take what is not yours' and that is a very important factor."

Myrna followed this up, asking; "Where did the money come from in the first place? How is that king's money earned? It could be taxes. It could be just going in, slaughtering people and taking what he wanted."

We discussed how this was similar to what went on in Mexico. We had heard about the maquilladores, the factories where people have to work seven days a week, twelve hour shifts, day in and day out. They are destroyed and yet earn very small wages. A lot of money is gained, but the workers are not getting it. The owners and large corporations are reaping big profits. If the workers complain or join groups such as the FAT (the worker's rights association), they are, like this man in the parable, denouncing what is not right and being punished.

When we have used this passage in Bible Study with other church groups, they have been surprised that this is not the passage about using talents. The last part of the parable is so shocking where it says, "to every person who has something, even more will be given; but the person who has nothing, even the little that he has will be taken away from him." It feels similar to what is happening now with the social programs being chipped away bit by bit. People are holding on by their fingernails and the little they have is going to be taken away.

So where is the hope?

Donna replied with great heaviness, "There isn't any. That is what is so depressing. Except for that one man who stood up and his very own words were used to condemn him. He is telling this bad king that he is taking away from people what does not belong to him."

Myrna interjected, "But if he said that in front of people to this king, then he is getting other people to think about what he said. He does not remain quiet. You are going to get people thinking about what is going on, but you will be in the owner's bad books. So that is what he did. The other people around would see what he did."

Elizabeth said, "He spoke up, but looked what happened. I don't like this parable."

Faye asked, "This is a parable. Why is Jesus telling it? Where is Jesus' word of hope in it?"

After a long, heavy silence Myrna replied; "Jesus is in the struggle of those people who stand up for what they believe. Every time we read this passage, we get something new out of it and it brings strength. This passage continues and goes on and on. It is not just a story, but a continuation of people who are rich and how they keep people down. It goes on and we learn something every time we read it. Nelson Mandela could have retracted and got out of jail, but he held on for all those years. The people remember that. The Jewish people have suffered so much over the years and so many have died. But they continue to struggle and there is hope in that."

Elizabeth agreed and said, "That is where the hope is. It is in the man who stood up and spoke."

Faye added, "Jesus stood up again and again for the rights of the people. He confronted the system that made more poverty and abused the people. He got killed, but that doesn't mean there is no hope in it. The hope is not necessarily tied to success, but that it is enough to stand up. Sometimes it is all that you can do. Even if you can't win, there is something that happens when we take a stand."

"The hope goes on," Myrna declared. "The story went on after. Imagine the talking that must have gone after and how the story spread out!"

Our collective stories are so connected to this tough parable and we have now seen it as a reality check and a challenge to never use the word "hope" lightly.

## Changes in the Women's Collective

Over the past two years we have talked, written, shared our stories and dug deep into our past experiences within our families, our community and the groups we are involved in that are working for social change. Our dialogues and seeing our own words in print has had a profound impact on us all. At the end of this work together, we decided to talk about what we have learned together and the effect that the writing of this book has had on each of us.

For all of us it has been an overwhelming experience. We feel very close to one another and have shared things we have never spoken of before. We all excitedly jumped in with how we have been affected by our work together and how important it has been for us. There were comments that we feel important now and that we have come to realize in new ways the importance of the work we have been doing in the community over the years. We have seen the connection between everything we do — our family, work, worship, projects and the life of the community.

We have also been changed by our writing together. Elizabeth said; "I am talking more now. I am not afraid to any more. I am talking out more than I ever thought I would. My heart used to pound when I was speaking and it doesn't any more. The two years working on the book have helped."

Melissa talked about how different the experience was than she thought it would be and that she (like the rest of us) didn't think we would still be at it two years later. She said; "I feel more educated now. We are opening our eyes to things around us that we never thought about before. I found that my family is educated more since I have been involved in the book. I never talked about what I did, but slowly now I talk more about it, because of the book. I was worried about how people in the community would respond to it. I think we have spoken very honestly. We were worried about people being degraded, but I think that what comes through is the strength of the community. So I am not worried about it now."

Myrna commented that a few weeks ago she got up in the middle of the night and wrote down her feelings about writing this book together. We urged her to share her thoughts with us and this is an excerpt from her writing:

> When we talked about this project, it was a dream. I often wondered as I was growing up what it would be like to write a book or for that matter have anything to do with one. I used to think how smart a person is to be able to write something people will read. Then when the idea came up, it was still a dream. A wonderful idea, but what could I possibly write about? Even as we worked, the other women and myself, I never could see who would want to hear our stories.
>
> As we worked together and our lives went down on paper, it wasn't just all talk. We all lived those stories. We felt each other's pain, sorrow and happiness. How each of us had respect for each other and our community and families. As we wrote down the stories, they were real. Out of the paper came a reinforcement that gave us such courage and hope. I hope our stories do get published. Maybe other women will get hope and strength to carry on to make our community and world a better place to live.
>
> What amazes me is how everything we have written about makes the circle of life. Even my hard times, the struggles, friendships, all go together. It would be nice to have a perfect world, but we have wonderful people. We just have to open our eyes to see.

Through our writing collective, our eyes have been opened to new insights about our work and struggle. The circle goes around, as Myrna often says — an intertwining spiral of experience, analysis, action and reflection. At the core of it all is the powerful sense of the presence of God who is with us in the midst of the struggle.

It is not by chance that we are a group of women who have gathered as a collective to discuss and reflect on our work for social change. We are the primary victims of poverty. We live and deal daily with the life-destroying effects of poverty on our children and families. We have taken on a responsibility to try to change society, to stand up to violence and abuse, to create places where we and our neighbours can learn, to create good jobs that pay fair wages and are good for our community. In all this struggle we have found a hope that gives life meaning and that has been at the root of all that has helped to build our community. That hope is everything!

# Notes

1    "Footsteps in the Sand"
One night I had a dream. I was walking along the beach with the Lord... The Lord said; "My child, I never left you. During your times of trial where you see only one set of footprints, I was carrying you." Margaret Fishback Powers, "Footprints," ©1993, HarperCollins, Toronto.

2    See Chapter 4, "The workers in the vineyard," pp. 64-65.

3    Wakin, Edward, *Monday Morality — Right and Wrong in Daily Life*, Paulist Press, New York, 1980.

4    The United Church of Canada provided seed funding for this mobile clinic.

5    Grants received for the Point Adult Centre for Education: — PLURA (Ecumenical coalition of the **P**resbyterian, **L**utheran, **U**nited, **R**oman Catholic, & **A**nglican churches for grassroots groups engaged in social justice), Quebec Ministry of Education, Community Clinic of Point St. Charles, Literacy Partners of Quebec, University Women's Club.

6    Elizabeth Garbish wrote the history of PACE for this book.

7    See Chapter 3, "Point Adult Centre for Education (PACE)," pp. 31-37.

8    See Chapter 3, "Women's Discussion Group," pp. 38-49.

9      See Chapter 3, "Point At Work (PAW)," pp. 50-58.

10      See Chapter 7, "Hope as the seed for transformation," pp. 130-135.

11      Waring, Marilyn, *If Women Counted — A New Feminist Economics*, Harper Collins, San Francisco, 1988.

12      St. Columba House 1994 Annual Report, p. 10 (b).

13      Soëlle, Dorothee with Shirley A. Cloyes, *To Work and To Love — a theology of creation*, Fortress Press, Philadelphia, 1984.

14      See Chapter 2, Rolly, pp. 21-22.

15      See Chapter 3, "Standing against abuse," pp. 41-42.

16      Luxton, Meg, "Two Hands for the Clock — Changing Patterns in the Gendered Division of Labour in the Home," in Meg Luxton, Harriet Rosenberg, and Sedef Arat-Koc, *Through the Kitchen Window — The Politics of Home and Family*, Garamond Press, Toronto, 1990.

17      See Chapter 5, "If women counted," pp. 86-91.

# Also of Interest from The United Church Publishing House

## Women and Religion

**Telling Her Story**
Theology out of Women's Struggles
*by Lois Miriam Wilson*
"I want to find a way to reconcile my profound love and debt to the biblical record with my emerging awareness of women's struggles towards wholeness. I want to communicate these learnings to children before they get any older." states Lois Wilson. Her popular book, now in its second printing, is an ideal resource for those who wish to bring new ears and eyes to biblical stories.
1-55134-000-3                                                        **Paper $7.95**

**Crucified Woman**
*by Doris Jean Dyke*
In this short and moving book, theologian Doris Dyke tells the powerful story of the impact the statue of a crucified woman, created by artist Almuth Lutkenhaus-Lackey, had on members of the church and university communities in downtown Toronto. For many, initial feelings of outrage evolved into new feelings and thoughts about traditional Christian doctrine and the suffering of women. *The Catholic New Times* praised the book, saying it "has the power to stay with you for a very long time."
0-919000-68-1                                                       **Paper $13.95**

**Images of Ourselves**
The Faith and Work of Canadian Women
*photos by Pamela Harris*
A book to celebrate The Ecumenical Decade of Churches in Solidarity with Women in Church and Society (1988-1998). *Images of Ourselves* is an acknowledgement and appreciation of the lives and work of women through prayer, poetry, song, meditation, and photography. Native women, farm women, city women, singles, young mothers, grandmothers, francophones, anglophones, church professionals, and volunteers from across the country and seven denominations have all contributed to this portrait of women's faith today. A powerful and challenging tool for devotion and renewal.
0919000-96-7                                                        **Paper $12.95**

# Social/Leadership Issues

## Leading Women
How Church Women Can Avoid Leadership Traps
and Negotiate the Gender Maze
*by Carol E. Becker*
This volume addresses the issues and concerns of the rapidly growing number of women in positions of church leadership. Author Carol Becker shows women how to communicate and influence decisions in a male world. She names the gender traps, examines the unique perspectives that women bring to leadership in the church, and explores communication strategies for women and men. Becker offers practical solutions for negotiating the gender maze for women working together with men in church leadership. Finally, she presents new paradigms for leadership to further the advancement of women in ministry.

**1-55134-049-6**                                                    **Paper $17.95**
**Canadian Rights Only**

## Embracing the Exile
A Lesbian Model of Pastoral Care
*by Sally M. Boyle*
Sally Boyle, lesbian-feminist and United Church hospital chaplain, leads us in a sensitive and challenging exploration of lesbian issues within the ever-expanding field of pastoral care. Boyle upholds lesbianism as a celebrated gift of sexuality and life through which the transforming power of God is revealed. Boyle's justice-based model of pastoral care employs acceptance, integration, transformation, and risk as ways to empower people to perform acts of justice. Challenging us to move beyond our own "isms," she promotes a methodology applicable to all who are moving towards wholeness, self-respect, and celebration.

**1-55134-047-X**                                                    **Paper $16.95**
**Co-published with artemis enterprises**

## Speaking for Themselves
Hearing the Gospel from the Dispossessed, the Undervalued
and the Marginalized
*by Clifford A.S. Elliott*
In this powerful and moving book, Clifford Elliott shares with us his gift of listening as he introduces eight remarkable people and their stories of pain, struggle and victory. You'll see how these people were able to grow from their experiences and find inner or spiritual strength. "An opportunity to listen to voices and stories not usually heard in mainstream communities."

**0-919000-62-2**                                                    **Paper $10.95**

# Women's Ministry

## Gathered by the River
Reflections and Essays of Women Doing Ministry
*edited by Gertrude Lebans*
This unique collection of essays, reflections, and prose brings to life the theology, struggles, and celebrations of women doing ministry. Introduced and edited by Gertrude Lebans, this ecumenical exploration of the changing face of ministry gives voice to the work of lay, diaconal and ordained women. A new vitality has been birthed as women minister through obstacles placed by the institutional church and patriarchal society. With passion and courage, women are initiating change as reflected by the critical insights and personal stories of the contributors.
1-55134-040-2                                        **Paper $16.95**
**Co-published with artemis enterprises**


## Petticoats in the Pulpit
The Story of Early Nineteenth-Century Methodist
Woman Preachers in Upper Canada
*by Elizabeth Gillan Muir*
The compelling story of the life and work of Methodist women who preached in the 1700s and 1800s in Canada, the U.S. and Britain. This look at the past, and the successes and frustrations of these talented women working in a society where they were barely tolerated, is an important addition to our knowledge of church history and an inspiration for female leadership today.
0-919000-78-9                                        **Paper $18.95**


## Crossing Worlds
The Story of the Woman's Missionary Society
of The United Church of Canada
*by Donna Sinclair*
For a generation of women across Canada, the code letters "WMS" opened up new worlds. Today the WMS remains a unique model of informed and action-oriented Christian community. Here was belonging, purpose, commitment, and the disciple of study, prayer, work, and giving. The result was a deep sense of connectedness. The dispossessed were no longer worlds away, there were known members of the family. A generation after the break point of 1962, remembering is a step toward renewal. In this book, our mothers-in-the-faith are speaking to us today.
0-919000-59-2                                        **Paper $10.95**

# Worship/Program Resources

## Joy Is Our Banquet
Resources for Everyday Worship
*by Keri K. Wehlander*

*Joy Is Our Banquet* is a timely, well-written resource for anyone involved in planning worship for small groups, retreats, committee meetings, or special events. Each of the liturgies is complete, with prayers, litanies, hymn suggestions, and biblical passages. The services are participatory and may be readily adapted for use in Sunday morning or other large group worship setting. The refreshing, sometimes startling, images contained in this resource highlight themes such as patience, friendship, beginnings, and money, affirming the everyday experiences that are an integral part of what is holy in life. This volume is poetic yet accessible, nurturing and giving expression to the spiritual journey of all who use it.

**1-55134-050-X**                                                **Spiral $14.95**

## There Is a Season
Fifty-eight Meditations for Private and Group Worship
*by Betty Radford Turcott*

The themes of justice, peace, and hope are explored in these fifty-eight inspirational devotions, which follow the church year. Each service is complete on two facing pages and includes a call to worship, opening prayer, scripture, suggested popular hymns, a brief meditation, and closing prayer. The services are suitable for both personal devotion and group worship. Those who have been asked to lead a worship service and have little or no time to prepare will find the help they need in this volume, which includes biblical reference and thematic indices.

**1-55134-039-9**                                                **Spiral $12.95**

## Program Ready II
More Quick and Complete Programs for the Church Year
*by Dorothy MacNeill*

Looking for MORE user-friendly material for your church group — but don't have time to prepare a program? Dorothy MacNeill's second collection offers all-new, ready material for worship, reflection, and discussion.

Each program is a complete service and includes a call to worship, prayers, hymn suggestions, and a short meditation, as well as ideas to spark group activities. These easily adapted sessions guide the user through celebrations from Advent and Epiphany to Lent and Easter, using themes that range from prayer, visiting and blessings, to flexibility, remembering and talent money.

*Program Ready II* is a welcome resource for those looking for more new and fresh ideas for women's groups, men's groups, Bible study groups, senior Sunday school, or youth groups. A valuable addition to any church or personal library for worship planning.

**1-55134-061-5**                                                **Spiral $12.95**

# Order Form
# The United Church Publishing House

**SHIP TO:**

Name: _______________________________________

Address: ____________________________________

_____________________________________________

Phone: ______________________________________

Fax: ________________________________________

| Title | ISBN number | Price | Copies | Total |
|---|---|---|---|---|
| Telling Her Story | 1-55134-000-3 | $7.95 | _____ | _____ |
| Crucified Woman | 0-919000-68-1 | $13.95 | _____ | _____ |
| Images of Ourselves | 0-919000-96-7 | $12.95 | _____ | _____ |
| Leading Women | 1-55134-049-6 | $17.95 | _____ | _____ |
| Embracing the Exile | 1-55134-047-X | $16.95 | _____ | _____ |
| Speaking for Themselves | 0-919000-62-2 | $10.95 | _____ | _____ |
| Gathered by the River | 1-55134-040-2 | $16.95 | _____ | _____ |
| Petticoats in the Pulpit | 0-919000-78-9 | $18.95 | _____ | _____ |
| Crossing Worlds | 0-919000-59-2 | $10.95 | _____ | _____ |
| Joy Is Our Banquet | 1-55134-050-X | $14.95 | _____ | _____ |
| There Is a Season | 1-55134-039-9 | $12.95 | _____ | _____ |
| Program Ready II | 1-55134-061-5 | $12.95 | _____ | _____ |
| Program Ready | 1-55134-037-2 | $10.95 | _____ | _____ |

**Subtotal** _____ _____

**Shipping Charges** $2.00 per book _____

**In Canada please add 7% GST** _____

**TOTAL** _____

Payment is required with your order. U.S. orders must be paid in U.S. funds. Thank you.

**Please mail your order with cheque to:**
The United Church Publishing House
Dept. P, 4th floor, 3250 Bloor St. W.
Etobicoke, Ontario, Canada, M8X 2Y4